CULTURE SMART!
POLAND

Greg Allen

Graphic Arts Center Publishing®

First published in Great Britain 2005
by Kuperard, an imprint of Bravo Ltd.

Series Editor Geoffrey Chesler
Design DW Design

Simultaneously published in the U.S.A. and Canada
by Graphic Arts Center Publishing Company
P. O. Box 10306, Portland, OR 97296-0306

Library of Congress Cataloging-in-Publication Data

Allen, Greg.
Poland: a quick guide to culture and etiquette / Greg Allen.
    p. cm. – (Culture smart!)
Includes bibliographical references and index.
ISBN 1-55868-846-3
1. Poland. I. Title. II. Series.
DK4040.A45 2004
943.8–dc22

                    2004020572

Printed in Hong Kong

Cover image: Market Square, Poznan.
Travel Ink/Phil Robinson

CultureShock!Consulting and **Culture Smart!** guides both contribute
to and regularly feature in the weekly travel program "Fast Track"
on BBC World TV.

About the Author

GREG ALLEN is the Canadian director of an intercultural management consultancy specializing in assisting Western businesspeople working in Poland. He obtained his MA in Sociology from Lancaster University, England, and is currently writing his Ph.D. thesis on intercultural management in Central and Eastern Europe. He has written extensively on the subject in academic journals. After moving to Poland in 1994, he now lives in a small town near Warsaw with his Polish wife and two daughters.

Other Books in the Series

Other titles are in preparation. For more information, contact: info@kuperard.co.uk

The publishers would like to thank **CultureShock!**Consulting for its help in researching and developing the concept for this series.

CultureShock!Consulting creates tailor-made seminars and consultancy programs to meet a wide range of corporate, public-sector, and individual needs. Whether delivering courses on multicultural team building in the U.S.A., preparing Chinese engineers for a posting in Europe, training call-center staff in India, or raising the awareness of Police Forces to the needs of diverse ethnic communities, we provide essential, practical, and powerful skills worldwide to an increasingly international workforce.

For details, visit www.cultureshockconsulting.com

contents

contents

Map of Poland

introduction

Culture Smart! guides set out to provide first-time
travelers with vital information about the values
and attitudes of the people they will meet, and
practical advice on how to make the most of their
visit abroad. Travelers to Poland in particular, a
country in rapid transition from its recent
Communist past, need to be open-minded and
well-informed. Despite sweeping changes to its
economic, cultural, and political landscape, the
essential spirit of Poland endures. The undulating
countryside, the passion and delicacy of Chopin,
and the crisp mornings of the golden Polish fall
continue to inspire Poles and visitors alike. Along
with a certain romanticism inherited from their
aristocracy, another product of Polish history has
been their stubborn resistance and pride, which
has often had dire consequences. Happily Poland
has turned a corner from its troubled past and is
now coming to grips with the new realities of
Europe and indeed of the modern world. Now is
a fascinating time to get to know Poland as it
reenters the European family.

Today's Poland is very much a mix of the old
and the new, and the two are not always in
harmony. *Culture Smart! Poland* provides a guide
to its lasting traditions, its Communist legacy, and

the latest trends. Background knowledge of the land, people, and history is crucial to an understanding of the Polish character: the Polish sense of identity has been forged by history, and the reader is introduced to the main events of Poland's turbulent past. The chapter on values and attitudes provides essential insights into this relationship-based society, and will prepare you for the specific nature of Polish social and business life. Other chapters show you where and how to meet local people and establish good relations, how Poles behave in everyday life, and how they celebrate special occasions. There are tips on coping with linguistic hurdles and how to negotiate the transportation infrastructure. Finally, the business chapter provides key information aimed at making your time in Poland as successful as it will be enjoyable.

More than anything else, the Polish people are warm and generous and place great value on personal relationships. Do not pass up the opportunity to visit people in their homes, as their hospitality is legendary. The Poles say, "A guest in the home is God in the home." *Culture Smart! Poland* will help you to become a better visitor and a welcome guest in their country.

Key Facts

Official Name	The Republic of Poland (*Rzeczpospolita Polska*)	
Capital City	Warsaw (Warszawa)	Population 1, 609, 608
Other Major Cities	Krakow, Lodz, Wroclaw, Poznan, Gdansk	
Borders	Belarus, Czech Republic, Germany, Lithuania, Russia (Kaliningrad enclave), Slovakia, Ukraine	
Area	120,628 sq. miles (312,700 sq. km)	Slightly smaller than Germany
Climate	Continental, with small moderating influence from the Baltic Sea in the North	
Currency	Zloty (PLN) 1 zloty=100 groszy	
Population	38,646,000 (2001)	63% Urban population
Ethnic Makeup	Polish 97.6%, German 1.3%, Ukrainian 0.6%, Belorussian 0.5%	
Language	Polish	Russian, English, and German are popular second languages.
Religion	Roman Catholic 95%	Eastern Orthodox, Protestant, and other 5%

Government	Parliamentary Republic. The Head of State is the President. Parliament has two chambers: the Sejm and Senat.	
Media	Television and radio are mixed private and public. The state broadcasters are Polskie Radio and Telewizja Polska.	The leading newspapers are *Gazeta Wyborcza*, *Rzeczpospolita*, and *Super Express* (tabloid).
Media: English Language	The *Warsaw Voice*, *Warsaw Business Journal*, *Warsaw Insider*	Foreign newspapers can be bought at kiosks in large cities.
Electricity	220 volts, 50 Hz (standard for continental Europe)	Buy adapters for U.S. appliances before traveling.
Video/TV	PAL/SECAM (standard for continental Europe)	
Telephone	The country code for Poland is 48. The Warsaw area code is 22.	For long-distance calling from Poland, dial 0 then the country code.
Time Zone	Central European (CET). One hour ahead of Greenwich Mean Time (G.M.T. +1). Six hours ahead of U.S. Eastern Standard Time (E.S.T.+ 6)	

LAND &
PEOPLE

Welcome to Poland, the historical bridge between East and West at the heart of Europe. Poland is a relatively large European country, with an area of 120,628 square miles (312,700 sq. km); it is slightly smaller than Germany and slightly larger than Italy. Its population of 38.6 million makes it the sixth most populous of the European Union's twenty-five member states.

Poland is a land of contrasts. A new member of the European Union with a growing, increasingly high-tech economy, it still has a massive agricultural sector in which farming methods have changed little over the centuries. The long Baltic coast to the north gives way to a wide central plain, and in the south are the rocky peaks of the Tatry Mountains. The large cities, such as Warsaw, Krakow, Gdansk, and Wroclaw, with their bright lights, modern facilities, and nightlife are in stark contrast to the backward villages of the countryside where life can appear to have stood still for a hundred years. The youth of Poland have embraced a modern, Western lifestyle, while much of the older generation remains very traditional. Even the climate is one of contrasts, with hot summers and cold, snowy winters. This contrast exists not only on a macro scale but also in individuals. Among the educated youth a strong sense of tradition persists, and even the most traditional Poles know how to enjoy themselves when the occasion calls for it.

Walking through the center of Warsaw today, it is hard to believe that not so long ago this was the capital of a bankrupt Communist state. Polish city centers are full of shops, boutiques, cafés, restaurants, pubs, and clubs. The cafés of Krakow and Wroclaw are every bit as charming and distinctive as those of Paris or Madrid. This is in stark contrast, however, to the rural countryside. While many of Poland's large cities have enjoyed the fruits of the recent growth of a free market economy, the countryside has not. In many small villages little has changed in the past twenty years, except for a slide into neglect and the migration of the youth to larger towns and cities.

Never feel shy about asking Poles to describe the changes that have transformed their country and society. In fact, there is often no need to ask, as many Poles are just as keen to share their views on the country as they are to hear a foreigner's.

GEOGRAPHICAL OVERVIEW

Poland is bordered to the west by Germany, to the south by the Czech and Slovak Republics, to the east by the Ukraine, Belarus, and Lithuania, and to the northeast by the tiny Russian enclave of Kaliningrad. The Baltic Sea defines the northern border.

The country is dominated by a large, central plain that encompasses the cities of Warsaw, Poznan, and Lodz. The port city of Gdansk is located on the Baltic. The entire southern part of the country is mountainous, with the highest peaks of the Tatry Mountains, 70 miles (113 km) south of Krakow, reaching an elevation of 8,200 feet (2,499 m). Two major rivers, the Vistula (*Wisla*) and the Oder (*Odra*), flow from the mountains in the south to the Baltic. The cities of Warsaw, Krakow, and Gdansk were built along the Vistula. The Oder forms a large part of the German–Polish border and has its mouth near the city of Szczecin in the northeast.

Major population centers are spread throughout the country, with Warsaw lying near the middle of the central plain, geographically isolated from any notable topographic features. Due west of Warsaw, approximately 200 miles (322 km) on the road to Berlin, is Poznan. Gdansk on the Baltic coast lies alongside Gdynia and Sopot; collectively they are known as the tri-city.

Krakow is situated some 200 miles south of Warsaw, just north of the Tatry Mountains. Wroclaw is located in the southwest of the country, north of the Sudety Mountains, which  continue into the Czech Republic and eastern Germany.

Climate

Poland has a primarily continental climate, tempered by the Baltic Sea in the north. Summers are typically hot and sunny, and the time when city residents flee in droves to the countryside, lakes, seaside, or mountains. In fact, Warsaw in the middle of summer can feel like a ghost town, deserted but for the tourists wandering around. The hot weather normally lasts from late May till early September, although this varies greatly from year to year.

Fall can range from dark and gloomy to stunningly beautiful. The famous Polish golden autumn has a deserved reputation. Perhaps the best words to describe Warsaw winters are gray and wet. These are in stark contrast to the snowy peaks of the mountainous south where the food, hospitality, and mulled beer should not be missed!

Average Daily Temperatures For Selected Months		
Warsaw	Fahrenheit	Celsius
January	27°	-2 °
April	46°	7 °
July	67°	19°
October	48°	9°

A BRIEF HISTORY

*"To be defeated and not submit, that
is victory; to be victorious and rest on
one's laurels, that is defeat."*

Jozef Pilsudski (1867–1935),
Polish commander-in-chief and statesman

Few countries have ever been more fought over
than Poland. The Russians, Prussians, Tatars,
Turks, Swedes, Austrians, and Germans have all
battled over this land. That the Polish nation
exists at all today is a testament to the resilience
and character of its people.

History shapes the mind-set of any nation,
but this point has a special significance in the
case of Poland. The suppression of their culture,
traditions, religion, and language in various
periods of their history has had a strong effect
on the way Poles view themselves and their
relations with others. From their checkered past

has come the Poles' indomitable spirit. They have lost many battles but not the war, and their vibrant culture and economy are proof of this.

Today's Poles are very conscious of their history and take great pride in their heritage and culture, which has been interwoven with the Catholic Church. Their national identity has largely been forged by the Church, which continues to be very influential in modern Polish society.

The Polish perception of their own history is far from objective, however. They prefer to focus on and take inspiration from the resilience of their ancestors and the continuity of their culture through the centuries. This has had the effect of turning Poland into an introverted nation, all too often detached, politically and psychologically, from the rest of the continent.

Through the prism of their history, the Poles see themselves as a strong, noble nation that has consistently been on the morally correct side of conflicts, if not always the victorious side. This has contributed to a self-image of victimhood. Rather than expecting support from beyond their borders, Poles learned to cope alone as best they could. Even today, foreigners in Poland are often told how the rest of the world has consistently abandoned Poland in its time of need.

The following section introduces some of the
most important developments in the history of
the Polish nation.

Origins

Little is known about the origins of the earliest
inhabitants of Poland. It is believed that they were
a mixture of hunter-gatherers and farmers who
helped develop the first trading routes through
the region. The remains of a sixth-century BCE
settlement, Biskupin, were unearthed in the 1930s
and can be seen today. This trade included the
Amber Road, dating back to the fifth century BCE,
linking the Baltic Sea to Rome and the
Mediterranean.

In the last years of the first millennium BCE
Celtic and Germanic tribes, among others,
started launching raids into the region. In
response to these attacks, the native settlers and
nomads began to organize themselves into
larger groups. One of these groups was the
Slavs, who are believed to have first arrived in
the territory of modern-
day Poland in the sixth
or seventh century CE.
They had migrated west
from the area of Belarus
while other Slavic tribes
moved south and east.

Being outside the Roman Empire, the peoples of the area were less advanced than their neighbors to the south and west. Nevertheless, they organized themselves into tribal communities with clear power structures, administrative centers, and trading settlements. The Slavs of the region thrived with the increase in trade and one of these groups, the Polanie, eventually settled in the central plain of modern-day Poland and laid the foundations of what would become the Polish nation.

The Piast Dynasty

From the ninth century, the Polanie were ruled by the Piast dynasty, which marks the beginnings of a Polish nation. Under Piast rule, Polish language and culture began to flourish.

Christianity came in 966 CE with the baptism of the Piast prince, Mieszko I. Mieszko wisely chose to accept Christianity directly from Rome, and thereby avoided the forced conversion of his pagan people at the hands of the Frankish German Empire. The Polish Church was established in the year 1000, directly under the control and protection of Rome. The first Polish King, Boleslaw the Brave, was crowned twenty-five years later, thus establishing the Kingdom of Poland.

In an incident bearing a striking similarity to the later assassination of Thomas à Becket at the behest of King Henry II of England, Stanislaw, the Bishop of Krakow, was murdered in 1079 on behalf of King Boleslaw II. This followed a series of uprisings against Boleslaw's rule in which Stanislaw took a leading role. These events set a precedent of the Church finding itself at odds with the ruling power of the time, which was to recur through the centuries, often with dire consequences.

In the year 1226, Duke Konrad of Mazovia, who was under attack from pagan Baltic tribes, requested assistance from the Teutonic Knights, a German Christian military order who were to have a significant and lasting influence on Poland. The Knights eventually turned on the Poles and gained control over the area of Prussia, depriving Poland of access to the sea. Their impressive architectural skills culminated in the massive castle in Marienburg, present-day Malbork, a tourist destination not to be missed! In addition, the port of Gdansk (Danzig), which had previously been controlled by a local Slav dynasty, was conquered and subsequently developed in this period. In taking Gdansk, the Teutonic Knights slaughtered the local population and invited German settlers into the city.

The Tatar Invasions

Another great but devastating foreign influence came from the Tatars, who first invaded Poland in 1241. The Tatars were nomadic Mongolian warriors from Central Asia, feared for their equestrian and archery skills. Although they owed allegiance to Genghis Khan, the Tatars operated independently, launching raids into Russian, Polish, Czech, and Hungarian territory and returning with their spoils to the steppe lands of Central Asia.

The invasions were swift and destructive. Villages were plundered and burned, and those who could fled far from their homes. Polish defenses proved no match for these skilled horsemen, and the great Polish cities of Legnica and Krakow were destroyed.

The rebuilding process that followed the Tatar invasions saw the development of a number of towns that were largely inhabited by foreign settlers. Germans introduced their own culture and traditions as well as their skills in a variety of trades. Another minority group that grew in size during this period was the Jews. They contributed to the economic growth of the kingdom despite the Church's displeasure at the tolerance shown them by the king, Boleslaw the Pious, who granted them a royal charter in 1264.

Kazimierz the Great

Toward the end of the Piast dynasty, Krakow flourished as the capital under King Kazimierz III (1333–70). Better known as Kazimierz the Great, he was to be the last of the Piast kings. It was in this period that one of Europe's first universities was established in Krakow. It still exists today as the Jagiellonian University, one of the country's most prestigious academic institutions.

The year 1331 saw the first sitting of the Polish parliament. Kazimierz III greatly extended Poland's borders and oversaw the writing of the country's first legal code. The country, and Krakow in particular, thrived thanks largely to the bustling east-west and north-south trade routes that crossed through Poland. It is said that Kazimierz "found Poland built of wood and left her built of stone."

The Jagiellonian Dynasty (1386–1572)

Without a male heir, Kazimierz the Great left the throne to his nephew, Louis the Great of Hungary. After much confusion as to who should sit on the Polish throne, Louis's crown eventually passed to his eleven-year-old daughter, Jadwiga, in 1384. Jadwiga wed the Grand Duke of Lithuania, Jagiello, in 1386, who accepted Christianity on behalf of his nation and was baptized as Wladyslaw II Jagiello. This union acted to protect Lithuania from the

Teutonic Knights, whose mission it was to forcibly convert the pagan peoples of Eastern Europe. The marriage marked the beginning of the Polish-Lithuanian union, perhaps the only successful such union in Polish history, and created what was the largest country in Europe. This union helped to keep the Tatars and Teutonic Knights at bay, while extending the Kingdom's borders from the Baltic to the Black Sea.

The Battle of Grunwald (Tannenberg)
Mongol invasions plagued Poland through the thirteenth century, but in the fifteenth century a group of Tatars came to Poland's aid. In the summer of 1410, Jagiello led a mixed army of Poles, Lithuanians, Orthodox Christians, Tatars, and Bohemian Hussites to a long-awaited victory over the Teutonic Knights in the battle of Grunwald. The German Order had enlisted the help of various Western European countries to combat the "pagan" Lithuanians and their Polish supporters. In fact, many of the Lithuanians who took part in the battle of Grunwald had not yet embraced Christianity, not to mention the Muslim Tatar troops. Although they comprised a minority of the forces, for Poles Grunwald is a symbol of

victory in the face of oppression. Local villagers
armed with nothing more than wooden clubs
helped swell the numbers and joined in to defeat
the military might of the Teutonic Knights with
their superior weaponry and skills. Poland was
finally free of this menace and the subsequent
peace saw the Polish–Lithuanian Union increase
its share of the region, although the Teutonic
Knights were permitted to retain
their stronghold at Marienburg.

With Jagiellonians briefly
holding power concurrently in
Hungary and Bohemia as well as

Poland–Lithuania, the combined empire eventually
stretched from the Baltic to the Black Sea and came
within a stone's throw of Moscow. This massive
territory held within it a variety of ethnic groups
including Poles, Lithuanians, Estonians,
Ukrainians, Prussians, Muslim Tatars, and Jews.

Religious Tolerance

Poland was known as a land of religious tolerance,
where each group could practice its faith without
fear of persecution. Between the twelfth and
fifteenth centuries Jews came in large numbers
from the west—mostly from German lands and
Bohemia—escaping the persecution and
massacres that accompanied the Crusades and the
Black Death, and later following their expulsion

from Spain. Unlike the largely peasant Slavic population, they were city dwellers and craftsmen, and experienced in trade and fiscal matters. For these reasons Polish kings and princes encouraged them to settle and offered them protection. Occasioned by Poland's need for merchants and tradesmen, this influx resulted in a thriving Jewish community. Another ethnic minority, the Prussians, were given considerable autonomy in order to provide the skills needed to drive economic expansion.

The Renaissance in Poland

While the cultural explosion of the Renaissance for the most part passed neighboring Russia by, Polish arts and sciences flourished during this period, with many influential thinkers taking advantage of Poland's tolerance of ideas not supported by the Church. The sixteenth century was a "Golden Age" of cultural, academic, and economic activity. This period saw Nicholas Copernicus (Mikolaj Kopernik) publish *On the Revolutions of the Celestial Spheres*, postulating that the Earth revolved around the Sun. Polish art, architecture, and literature were strongly influenced by Renaissance Italy.

The Royal Republic

In 1569, the Polish Sejm, or Parliament, enacted the Union of Lublin, formally uniting Poland and Lithuania into the Polish Commonwealth. The period of Jagiellonian rule in Poland ended with Zygmunt August, who died in 1572 without an heir, and was followed by the so-called Republic of Nobles, which introduced elected succession, with the nobility electing the new king. Corruption reigned supreme in the process, with votes being openly bought and sold, resulting ultimately in a series of foreign rulers and sowing the seeds of the destruction of Poland as a strong, centralized European power. In a period when other European countries were moving toward more centralized government, Poland was governed by a feudal nobility and became increasingly regionally divided. The Poles were proving a difficult lot to govern and there was little allegiance to the elected monarchs, foreign or Polish.

There were, however, victories for the Polish army in this period, most notably the defeat of Ivan the Terrible of Russia. Stefan Batory of Transylvania, husband of Anna, who had temporarily held the throne until married, led Poland to battle over the contested land of Livonia (roughly modern-day Latvia) in 1571. Were it not for interference from Rome, Batory may well have taken Moscow, so complete was his victory over the Russians.

The third of the elected rulers, the Swedish Zygmunt III, moved the capital from Krakow to Warsaw in 1596, an act for which Krakovians have not forgiven him to this day.

The Reformation and Counter-Reformation.
It is a common misconception that the Catholic Church remained unchallenged in its spiritual domination of Poland throughout its thousand-year history in the country. By the middle of the sixteenth century, the Sejm was dominated by Protestant princes who had curtailed the power of the Church. As we have seen, Poland had adopted an official position of religious tolerance. This resulted, among other things, in Lutheran Livonia seeking Polish protection from Orthodox Russia. The region in return became Polish territory. With many of the Polish nobility having converted to Protestantism and with the Germanic regions of the country being strongly Lutheran, Poland looked to be following the lead of her Western neighbors on the road to becoming a Protestant nation. One key factor was missing, however. With no effective native professional or middle class of tradesmen and skilled workers, there was a dichotomy of classes

in Poland, which remained stubbornly entrenched in the feudal system.

This marks the beginning of a trend that was to have profound effects on Polish society throughout the following centuries. While a skilled and literate middle class was growing in countries to the West, no sizeable equivalent existed in Poland (hence the need to import skilled Jewish and German tradesmen). It was the urban middle class that was fueling the Reformation in the West, and this was lacking in Poland. The popularity of the reformist movement in Poland was almost exclusively an upper-class phenomenon, while the peasants remained loyal to the Catholic Church.

The Counter-Reformation was a largely bloodless victory for the Catholics. The Polish Church was reformed and Jesuits opened schools and helped to regain what trust the Church had previously lost. The defining moment came in 1564 when King Zygmunt (Sigmund) II, who had previously favored  Protestantism, was persuaded to accept the Catholic faith. Protestants were subsequently neither expelled nor persecuted. The official position of religious tolerance remained in place, although

Jesuits were encouraged to convert the remaining pockets of Protestantism. The Orthodox Cossacks of the Ukraine were also targeted for conversion, which was partly responsible for the Cossack uprising of 1648.

The position of the Catholic Church in Poland was strengthened in the second half of the seventeenth century when the Protestant Charles X of Sweden invaded the country, sacking churches and monasteries, and committing atrocities against the general population. These attacks were largely seen by the Polish population as being Protestant versus Catholic in nature, rather than as an opportunistic land grab.

Potop (The Deluge)

In 1648, the so-called *potop*, or deluge, began with Poland being attacked simultaneously by Swedes, Tatars, and Cossacks. Poland's vulnerable position was largely the result of petty infighting among the quarrelsome and proud nobility. This period of history has been immortalized, although in a rather nationalistic manner, in the epic novel *Potop* by Henryk Sienkiewicz (1846–1916). After the Swedes had completely ransacked most of the country, the Poles regrouped and mounted an impressive offensive to regain much of the lost territory. Poles would recall the *potop* frequently in their later history as an example of how they could turn the tables on foreign invasion and oppression.

Peace with Sweden was secured by the Treaty of Oliwa in 1660, but Poland–Lithuania lay in ruins with enemies across each border. The landmass of the Commonwealth was greatly diminished and nearly half the population had died through war and disease.

Arguably, Poland's finest hour militarily came in 1683 when King Jan III Sobieski convincingly defeated the Ottoman Turks as they made their way through the Balkans and on to Vienna. Many Poles still regard this as the moment they "saved" Christian Europe from Muslim rule. The Austrians, however, had an eye on Galicia in southern Poland and before long the two states would find themselves at war.

Back at home the Commonwealth continued crumbling due largely to nepotism, the inefficient political structure, and bitter infighting between groups of nobles. As central political power was further eroded, Poland's neighbors began to set their sights on her. Russia in particular, under the reigns of Peter the Great (1682–1725) and Catherine the Great (1762–96), increasingly exploited her divisions to gain influence in Warsaw.

The Partitions

For the period 1795–1916, Poland was absent from the map of Europe. In a series of three partitions, the enfeebled state was divided between Peter the Great's Russia, Frederick II's Kingdom of Prussia, and Maria Theresa's Austrian Empire. Each of these powerful empires had territorial ambitions and their weak and divided neighbor provided a tempting opportunity.

The first partition, in 1772, was a tactical move proposed by Frederick II to secure lands that Peter the Great had set his sights on, thereby avoiding a Russian–Austrian war. The three powers agreed to divide Poland in such a way that a balance would be achieved between them, and war averted. Under the first partition, the northern and central regions of Pomerelia and Ermeland were ceded to Prussia, Belarus and Latgale in the east to Russia, and the southern region of Galicia to Austria.

After losing about a third of Poland's territory and half its inhabitants in the first partition, King Stanislaw August together with the Sejm took steps toward political reform in an attempt to avoid losing control of more of the country. These reforms culminated in Europe's first written constitution, the second in the world following that of the U.S.A. The May 3 Constitution, as it was known, is still a source of pride for Poles and a national holiday marks the occasion.

Provoked by the constitution, Russia moved against the new government and instigated the second partition of Poland in 1793. This partition enlarged the Russian sector to the east and the Prussian sector to the west, including Gdansk, while leaving Poland with a small fragment of its former lands.

In an attempt to reclaim Polish honor after capitulation in the first two partitions, Tadeusz Kosciuszko led an army composed mainly of peasants armed with scythes against the Russian occupiers. Kosciuszko, a hero of the American War of Independence, and his peasant troops mounted an impressive offensive. It was never going to be enough to defeat the Russian forces, however. This insurrection gave Catherine the Great all the reason she needed to finish the process that had begun with the first partition and end the existence of the Polish state in 1795.

Napoleon Bonaparte
A brief respite from complete foreign domination came in the form of Napoleon Bonaparte. Recognizing that a victory for Napoleon over their occupiers would be the best chance for Poland to regain its independence, the Poles rallied behind the French emperor both at home

and abroad. For their support, the only independence they were granted, however, was the semi-autonomous Duchy of Warsaw, created in 1807 out of Polish lands Napoleon's troops had captured from the Prussians. As Napoleon's men retreated from the advancing Russians, the Duchy of Warsaw was quickly recaptured and put under Russian control.

The Congress of Vienna in 1815 offered little to Poles hoping for autonomy in part of what had been their vast country. The occupying powers reestablished their control. The Duchy of Warsaw was ceded to Russia as a semi-independent state called the Congress Kingdom of Poland, with the Russian Tsar as King of Poland. Krakow was made a "free city" within Austrian-held Galicia. Guarantees of home rule in all parts of the divided country, and of free communication between them, were given by all three occupying powers, only to prove empty.

Nationalism and Uprisings
The Poles constantly struggled for national liberation. The so-called November Uprising of 1830 against the Russian occupiers was centered in what had been the Duchy of Warsaw. The new Russian Tsar, Nicholas I, responded with a heavy hand, crushing the insurgents and enacting new

laws effectively outlawing Polish language and culture in an attempt to the Russianize the population. The inability of the intelligentsia to gain the support of the peasants in the countryside prevented the uprising from growing into a full-scale insurrection. Many of those who could emigrated in this period to escape a dire economic situation and intensified Russian oppression. The years 1846 and 1863 saw other failed insurrections, after which many insurgents were exiled to Siberia.

The Polish adage about the best coming out through suffering was proved true in this period. A cultural revival took place under this repressive occupation. Most notable examples were the composer Frédéric Chopin (1810–49) and the Romantic poets Adam Mickiewicz (1798–1855) and Juliusz Slowacki (1809–49). These artists drew on the plight of their nation as a source of inspiration, and are still held in extremely high regard.

The Industrial Revolution in Poland
The rise of capitalism and industrialization in the latter half of the nineteenth century had profound effects on Polish society. One of these was a mass migration to the cities, as peasants left the land

and sought work in the growing number of factories and coal mines. The cities of Katowice and Lodz developed in this period. The mobility and growing power of the peasants undermined the power and influence of the Polish nobility, who increasingly left their estates for the cities.

Millions of Poles emigrated in this period, mainly to the U.S.A., in search of a life without the economic hardships and political oppression of their homeland. In 1892 the National Polish Socialist Party was founded by Jozef Pilsudski.

The First World War

The First World War was devastating for each of the three powers occupying Poland. As much of the fighting took place on Polish soil, it was devastating for Poland as well, with an estimated one million Poles dead by the war's end. The war did, however, provide the opportunity for Poland to become a sovereign state once again. At the insistence of U.S. President Woodrow Wilson, the postwar settlement was based upon the principle of national self-determination. In 1918 an independent Polish republic was established, with Marshal Pilsudski elected as president.

Following the Treaty of Versailles in 1919, the newly drawn borders of Poland resulted in East Prussia being cut off from Germany by the so-called "Polish corridor," giving Poland access to the Baltic. The port of Gdansk, or Danzig as the Germans referred to it, was given the status of a free, trading city-state. The population of Gdansk remained predominantly German. The Polish Constitution of 1921 protected the rights of national minorities.

The Polish-Soviet War
With Lenin looking to spread Marxism westward and Marshal Pilsudski aiming to regain historic Polish territory in the east, war was inevitable. In 1919–21 Polish forces advanced into newly independent Lithuania, seizing control of its capital Vilnius, and into the Ukraine as far as Kiev. Then Poland's own independence came under threat as the Red Army approached to within a few miles of Warsaw. Pilsudski's August, 1920 counteroffensive, known as "the miracle on the Vistula," however, drove it back over three hundred miles into the Ukraine. The subsequent peace, signed in Riga in 1921, saw Poland and Russia divide much of the Ukraine and Belarus between themselves. On its other front, Poland managed to keep Vilnius.

The Interwar Period

The period between the First and Second World Wars is regarded by many Poles as the country's cultural coming of age, and an age that was stolen from them by the events that were to follow. Warsaw residents in particular are fond of telling stories of their city's international appeal during this all-too-brief period of peace and prosperity.

The first parliamentary governments of the Polish Republic consisted of right-wing and centrist parties. They faced a country in ruins after six years of war and tried, unsuccessfully, to create a stable currency, jobs for millions of unemployed, and a *modus vivendi* with national minorities and neighboring states. There was widespread discontent and civil disorder. In 1926, Pilsudski, frustrated by the incompetence of Parliament, seized full power in a military coup, effectively making Poland a military dictatorship. He had the support of his people, however, and under his direction the economy was revived and the country, divided for so long, began to rebuild itself. On his death in 1935, a military regime held power under Marshal Smigly-Rydz.

Rising feelings of nationalism further strained relations between Poles and their minority communities. Poland had Europe's largest Jewish population, numbering 3.5 million souls. Unease over the Nazi persecution of German Jews was tangible, and worried not only Poland's Jews but also many Poles who feared the German *Führer* would not tolerate a massive Jewish presence in his backyard and would use this as a pretext for aggression. In the late 1930s a wave of anti-Jewish pogroms swept Poland, and boycotts were organized against Jewish businesses. Many Polish liberals honorably provided moral and political support for the Jews in this difficult time.

Dark clouds were gathering on the horizon. Poland was flanked by two countries ruled by aggressive dictators: Stalin to the east and Hitler to the south and west, following the annexation of Czechoslovakia in May, 1938. Ominously, Stalin and Hitler had secretly signed a nonaggression pact by which, theoretically at least, each party was free to invade Poland from its respective side without fear of interference from the other. With Poland thus surrounded and Hitler's concept of *Lebensraum* already being put into practice, there was only one outcome.

The Second World War

On September 1, 1939, Hitler used the Polish refusal to renegotiate the status of Danzig and East Prussia as an excuse to launch war against his eastern neighbor. Two weeks later the Soviets invaded Poland from the east, and by the month's end the country was once again under complete foreign domination. In support of Poland, England and France declared war on Germany, but offered no immediate military support to the beleaguered Poles.

While the Nazi German enslavement and slaughter of prisoners of war is well documented, many are unaware that an estimated 1,660,000 Polish soldiers and civilians were deported to labor camps by the Soviets in 1940 and 1941. Additionally, thousands of prisoners of war were executed by the Red Army as part of their agreement with Hitler to wipe the Polish state off the map of Europe. Most notorious among such incidents was the execution of over 4,000 officers of the defeated Polish army in the forests of Katyn in March 1940. The refusal of the Soviet authorities to accept responsibility or even acknowledge the massacre was a cause of great animosity among ordinary Poles.

Germany gained complete control of Polish territory after invading the Soviet Union in June 1941. A system of concentration camps, such as Auschwitz and Treblinka, was set up by the Germans—well outside their own borders—to rid themselves of "racial inferiors" in their newly conquered lands. These death factories served both to supply slave labor for the war effort and to exterminate millions in gas chambers and by other means.

THE WARSAW GHETTO

In 1939 the Nazis established a ghetto in the
center of Warsaw into which 433,000 Jews
were crowded. In 1942 transports to the
extermination camp at Treblinka began. In
April 1943 the SS were sent in to round up the
remaining Jews and destroy the buildings.
Rather than submit, the Jews fought back
with small arms they had managed to
smuggle in. Resistance continued until May.
Many Jewish fighters escaped via the sewers
and joined the Polish underground.

The Warsaw Uprising
When Germany attacked the Soviet Union in
1941, the Poles and Soviets suddenly shared a
common enemy. Far from becoming close allies,
however, Soviet troops sat just across the Vistula
from central Warsaw and watched as the
Germans brought down the Warsaw Uprising of
1944. Coordinated by the pro-Western Polish
Home Army, known as the Armija Krajowa,
with a mandate from the Polish Government-in-
Exile in London, the uprising had begun on
August 1, when the Soviet Army was advancing
toward the capital. It ended as a massacre. The
Western Allies put little pressure on the Soviets
to help the Poles, and Stalin vetoed the Allied

use of his airfields for supply drops. After sixty-three days of bitter fighting some 200,000 Poles were killed. In retaliation the Germans razed the city, leaving nothing but piles of rubble, before fleeing. The Red Army eventually liberated Poland from the Nazis in 1945. By the end of the war, 6 million Polish citizens had died, half of them Jews.

The Postwar Settlement

At the Yalta Conference in February 1945, Stalin gained assurances from Roosevelt and Churchill that Poland would be left in the Soviet sphere of influence. After all their suffering in the war, Poles felt betrayed by their Western allies.

Following Yalta, and the Potsdam Conferences in July/August 1945, it was decided that Poland would be returned to its approximate medieval boundaries, meaning a general shift to the west of some 120 miles (193 km). Western territory was taken from Germany and eastern lands were given to the Soviet Union. This operation involved the forced mass migration of approximately 3 million Poles and 2 million Germans. The results can still be seen today in cities such as Wroclaw (formerly Breslau), where the German population was completely replaced by Poles, mostly from the region of modern-day Ukraine.

Communism

Poland was always far from being the ideal
Communist state. Stalin is said to have referred to
Polish Communists as resembling radishes: red on
the outside, but scratch a little and inside they're
pure white.

It was no surprise when, in
1946, the Communists were
given the green light to
nationalize the country's
economy in the rigged "three

times yes" referendum. The following year all
right-wing political parties were outlawed and a
socialist coalition was formed to govern the
People's Republic of Poland with no real
opposition. The People's Republic marched more
or less in step with Moscow, and Polish citizens
didn't have to live with secret police oppression
on the scale of the East German Stasi or Russia's
KGB. By 1949 the (Communist) Polish United
Worker's Party (PZPR) had become the only
political force in the country.

In 1949 Poland joined Comecon, the Soviet-
dominated economic bloc. The early 1950s saw
the introduction of harsh Stalinist rule, including
further nationalization, rural collectivization, and
persecution of members of the Church. In 1955
Poland joined the Warsaw Pact Soviet defense
organization.

The imposition of Stalinism, however, had the effect of driving Poles toward the Catholic Church, which was effectively the only organization outside Communist control allowed by the government. There were strikes and riots in Poznan in 1956, and in the 1960s a small measure of liberalization took place. The economy languished, however, and in 1970 there were riots in Gdansk against food price rises.

The first mass signs of discontent with the Communist system could perhaps be seen at the widespread jubilation at the election of Karol Wojtyla as Pope John Paul II in 1978. When the new Pope visited his homeland a year later, he was greeted by the largest public gathering of Poles in history. The Catholic Church, which had always provided a discreet counterpoint to Communist propaganda, had suddenly come to the fore as a political force in the country.

Solidarity and Martial Law

In 1980, a Gdansk shipyard electrician named Lech Walesa led a group of striking workers angered over the recent 100 percent rise in the price of foodstuffs. The Solidarity Trade Union was formed and supported striking miners in Silesia as well as the workers in the Baltic Sea port. The strikers gained popular support, including that of the Catholic Church and opposition intellectuals. The group's demands, or twenty-one points, listed the rights that were soon being fought for throughout the Eastern bloc. By June 1980, the government had officially recognized Solidarity and made concessions to the workers.

After giving in and granting official recognition to Solidarity, the Polish government, under intense pressure from Moscow, reversed this decision. In December 1981, under the leadership of General Jaruzelski, martial law was declared. With their new sweeping powers, military police rounded up and imprisoned Solidarity leaders and activists, including Walesa, and the trade union was officially disbanded. During this period civil liberties virtually ceased to exist. Tanks rumbled through the streets, roadblocks sprang up as all traffic was searched, and thousands were detained without being formally charged.

By 1982, the government hoped it had sufficiently slowed the momentum of Solidarity. Walesa was freed and the following year martial law was lifted. Their hopes were in vain, however, as Walesa was to receive the Nobel Peace Prize in the same year, giving international recognition and sympathy to his struggling organization. Back home meanwhile, the murder of Father Jerzy Popieluszko, a Solidarity sympathizer, by a secret policeman did little to rebuild trust in the beleaguered government.

At the same time as Jaruzelski was losing the struggle for popular support to Solidarity, the country was facing possibly its most severe financial crisis. Because it was on the brink of bankruptcy, all goods produced were exported for hard, Western currency, leaving precious little for domestic consumption. Any Pole who lived through the 1980s remembers this period as a time of rationing and scarcity. Lines outside shops wound around city blocks, and many still recall rows of shelves with nothing on them but a few bottles of vinegar.

To maintain a decent standard of life in this period, many relied on informal networks of friends and acquaintances to acquire officially contraband goods. Such networks survive to this day and, in many cases, help to explain the way business dealings can work in this country.

The Fall of Communism

By the late 1980s, the desperate economic state of its citizens, coupled with the wind of political change blowing through Central and Eastern Europe, spelled the end for the Communist regime in Poland. In a last gasp attempt to reach a compromise and avoid anarchy, General Jaruzelski invited representatives of Solidarity, including Lech Walesa, to participate in a series of roundtable talks. The result was a compromise

under which Solidarity would
be legally recognized, and
permitted to have its
candidates contest a limited
number of seats in

parliamentary elections. The writing was on the
wall for the government when Solidarity
candidates cruised through to easy victories in
nearly all the contested seats.

For members of the Communist Party, it was a
case of jumping from a sinking ship, and in 1989
the popular journalist and Solidarity advisor
Tadeusz Mazowiecki was chosen to lead an
interim government to oversee open presidential
elections the following year. Once again in the
political spotlight, Lech Walesa easily won the
elections, becoming Poland's first post-
Communist president.

The following years were difficult for most
Poles as tough austerity measures took their toll,
but the atmosphere was one of change and, for
the most part, people were prepared to suffer
today for the promise of a better tomorrow. The
entrepreneurial spirit in the country began to
show as seemingly everyone who could became
involved in some form of business. This ranged
from the setting up of local subsidiaries of
prestigious Western firms, to selling homegrown
produce from the trunk of a car.

To the Present

Poland's economic growth has been surprisingly stable and the country has managed to avoid the economic crises that have afflicted many other Central European countries. Despite this, much of the enthusiasm of the early 1990s waned as the reform and privatization programs became mired in allegations of sleaze and corruption and the black and gray economies thrived. Much hope was placed in European Union integration as a cure for the economic ills of the country.

ETHNIC GROUPS

For most of its history, Poland consisted of a mix of different ethnic groups, including Jews, Germans, Russians, Byelorussians, and Ukrainians. Each left its mark on Polish history and culture, but today the country is devoid of any sizeable minority community.

At present, ethnic Poles make up 98 percent of the population, with Germans being the largest ethnic minority. The Jewish population of 3.5 million was wiped out in the Holocaust. Most who survived emigrated to Israel or the United States. The shifting borders of the post-Second World War settlement resulted in the expulsion of 2 million Germans from Polish territory, while Poland's eastern fringe, which had largely been inhabited by

Ukrainians, Byelorussians, and Lithuanians,
became part of the Soviet Union. In the same
period, some 3 million ethnic Poles were
repatriated from the Soviet Union.

THE INTELLIGENTSIA

The traditions of the landed gentry feature
strongly in Polish folklore, and the descendants of
these nobles are still extremely proud of their
lineage. There exists a romantic image of nobles,
often penniless, riding to and from each other's
estates and enjoying the hospitality of their hosts.
At the opposite end of the spectrum were the
serfs, whose lot in life seems to have been
overlooked by the folktales.

During the period of foreign occupation, this
landed upper class developed into what would
come to be known as the intelligentsia, an
educated elite. They led the Polish cultural and
political resistance throughout the years of
partition and established an unofficial
government-in-exile in nineteenth-century Paris,
keeping alive the dream of a proud, free Polish
nation. With the return of independence at the
end of the First World War, the intelligentsia
helped guide the nation as the torchbearers of the
culture and heritage of their ancestors.

The Second World War was disastrous for the

intelligentsia; both the Soviets and the Nazis marked them out for deportation to labor camps or for execution in an attempt to deprive the country of its greatest source of inspiration and leadership.

The postwar Communist government was eager to educate young, working-class Poles from the countryside, resulting in a greatly altered background to the new intelligentsia. Some supported the socialist system, and others would eventually join with Solidarity to fight the government's strict control. In so doing, the latter group followed in the footsteps of their predecessors by keeping alive the idea of an independent, western-looking Poland built on its traditional roots.

Since the fall of Communism, the intelligentsia has once again diversified and fragmented. The educated elite was for the most part economically protected under socialism. Today many intellectuals feel disenchanted and threatened by the impact of full-blooded capitalism, materialistic values, and consumerism. University professors working in the state system receive salaries on a par with an office assistant, all of which has led to a new brain drain, mainly of scientists, to Western Europe and North America. This Polish upper class, much like the nation itself, seems to be at its strongest when its country, along with her culture and traditions, is under threat.

POLAND'S CITIES

Warsaw

Poland's capital city is also the country's largest, with a population of over 1.6 million. Warsaw replaced Krakow as the Polish capital in 1596 due to its more central location in the Royal Republic of Poland–Lithuania that had been formed twenty-seven years earlier. Still centrally located within the country's post Second World War borders, Warsaw lies on the Vistula River and is the heart of modern Poland's commercial sector.

The failed 1944 Warsaw uprising against Nazi occupation resulted in the Germans reducing the historic core of the city to rubble. A massive postwar reconstruction project followed. The result of this is a charming old town painstakingly reconstructed to its original state and granted a place on Unesco's Cultural and Natural Heritage list. While the old town is an architectural gem, the rest of the city is a hodgepodge of styles ranging from original nineteenth-century palaces to row upon row of Communist-era blocks, to modern office towers.

Krakow

With a population of approximately 740,000, Krakow is Poland's third-largest city after Warsaw and Lodz. It is situated on the banks of the Vistula River, 200 miles (322 km) south of Warsaw and just north of the Tatry Mountains. Krakow's history dates back to the seventh century, with the Catholic Church establishing itself in the city in the year 1000. Thirty-eight years later, Krakow became the Polish capital under the Piast dynasty. Although the city has been invaded many times through the centuries it has remained relatively intact, and certainly fared better than Warsaw in the Second World War. The "cultural capital" of Poland is rich in historical sites, museums, and galleries.

Lodz

Poland's second-largest city (population 787,000) is centrally located, approximately 93 miles (150 km) southwest of Warsaw. The city is a product of the industrial revolution and built its wealth on textile factories, many of which were owned by Jews and Germans. The architecture consists largely of red-brick buildings mixed with the ubiquitous 1970s housing developments.

Wroclaw

A city of 634,000 inhabitants, Wroclaw is located on the Odra River in the southeast just north of the Sudety Mountains. Wroclaw, together with much of western Poland, was handed over to Poland after the Second World War by the Germans, to whom it was known as Breslau. Although largely destroyed by the Russians as they drove westward into central Germany, the city today bears little sign of this. Wroclaw rivals Krakow in its majestic beauty, although the latter holds a truer place in the hearts of most Poles.

Gdansk

Gdansk has been a strategically key city on the Baltic Sea for centuries. The port city has a population of 455,000, which jumps to approximately 800,000 when the nearby cities of Sopot and Gdynia (together known as the tri-city) are included. Gdansk has changed hands numerous times as well as holding the status of independent city-state. Its strategic importance both in commerce and battle has made it much fought over. The Second World War began in Gdansk on September 1, 1939, and more recently, Lech Walesa led its shipyard workers in a strike that was to mark the beginning of the Solidarity Trade Union.

A Tale of Two Capitals

"The big village" is how natives of Krakow describe Warsaw. They feel that the frenetic pace of life in the capital doesn't bear comparison with the more relaxed, cultured lifestyle of Krakow. For their part, most Warsaw residents hold no grudge against Krakow. They will openly admit that

Warsaw cannot match its beauty or history, but don't take it seriously as a place where business can be done or careers made.

Both of these stereotypes are rooted in some degree of reality. First of all, Warsaw can, at times, feel like a village. In the aftermath of the Second World War, with the capital a virtual ghost town, the government encouraged villagers from the surrounding countryside to take up residence in the city. This new labor force was put to work in the massive task of reconstruction as well as in the new factories that were sprouting up. Even today, it can be difficult to find a resident of Warsaw who was born and raised in the city. In the last decade there has been an influx of young people in search of employment or a high standard of postsecondary education. Companies in Warsaw often prefer hiring such people over locals as their financial expectations are lower and they tend to be more amenable to working long hours.

As for Krakow, residents still believe that they were robbed of their rightful status in 1596, when Zygmunt III moved the capital to Warsaw. It has certainly been left behind by the frantic pace of development set by Warsaw and attracts only a fraction of foreign investment in

the country. Salaries are notably lower than in the capital, but so too is the cost of living. It has, however, retained its place as Poland's cultural capital. The sheer number of treasures in Krakow is unmatched by any other Polish city. And on a sunny afternoon, the pavement cafés on its main square easily outshine Warsaw's crowded bars.

GOVERNMENT AND POLITICS

Since the first free elections were held on October 27, 1991, the Republic of Poland has been a parliamentary democracy with a structure very similar to that of many other European Union countries. The current workings of the government and presidency were set out in the Easter Constitution of October 1997.

The Presidency

The new constitution weakened the role of the president, but left intact certain executive powers. The president is commander-in-chief of the armed forces, has influence in appointing military and foreign policy officials, and can veto any bill, although this veto can be overruled by a three-fifths majority in Parliament.

Former Solidarity leader Lech Walesa won the first free presidential election, but quickly fell out of favor when he proved less competent in office than he had been in opposing the Communists. After being narrowly defeated by Aleksander Kwasniewski in 1995, he was humiliated by the incumbent five years later when he gained only 1.43 percent of the vote. Many Poles still regard Walesa with gratitude and fondness, but wish he had stepped out of the spotlight once the changes he had fought for had come into effect. Also his strong links with the Church and his blurring of Church-state separation contributed to his plummeting popularity.

Kwasniewski proved a much more popular president than his predecessor. Ironically, his diminished responsibilities under the 1997 constitution may have played a role in this, as the president is now less involved than before in divisive party political issues. He played the role of international statesman in a way that made many Poles feel proud of their country.

Having no party political ties is increasingly becoming an asset in Poland as the number of corruption scandals seems to grow each year, whichever government is in office. By and large, Poles have become disillusioned with the reform process and much of the enthusiasm of the 1990s has been replaced by indifference and scepticism.

The Parliament

The Polish Parliament is made up of two chambers: the Sejm (pronounced "same"), which has 460 members elected by proportional representation, and the Senate, made up of 100 senators, elected by a majority voting system. Unlike the presidency, which has a five-year term, both the Sejm and Senate are elected for four years. The minimum percentage of votes required for representation in the Sejm is 5 percent for individual parties and 8 percent for multiparty coalitions. Special exceptions to this rule are made for special-interest minority groups such as the ethnic German minority.

The position of prime minister has been a much less stable one than that of the president. From 1991 to 2004, Poland had eight prime ministers compared to only two presidents. Political parties are volatile as well. Although the same faces seem to stay in circulation, the actual parties and coalitions change frequently.

POLAND IN THE EUROPEAN UNION

The long process of Polish–E.U. integration brought to the surface many of the deep feelings and insecurities that Poles have about their place in Europe. They regard themselves as very much belonging to a Europe that predates the European

Union. They see their history, both the good and the bad, as being inexorably linked with that of Western Europe. While many Western Europeans think of the natural boundaries of Western Europe as being defined by the German–Polish border, many Poles see it lying on Poland's eastern border with Belarus and Ukraine.

E.U. membership is seen as a right and many were frustrated when Brussels and the founder states expected Poland to consider it a privilege. This position is deeply entrenched, and Poles react very negatively to being told what to do by the "West." A clear example was the reprimand by Jacques Chirac over Poland's failure to discuss its position with the E.U. before lending support to America in the run-up to the Iraq war. He suggested that there could be repercussions for Poland's E.U. candidacy if it continued to go against the grain of French-German policy. Despite the fact that most Poles did not support the government's Iraq policy, the reaction to Mr. Chirac was furious.

E.U. Membership Negotiations
Polish–European Union integration negotiations began as early as 1989 when the interim government of Tadeusz Mazowiecki held talks

with officials from the European Community.
These initial talks led to the birth of the E.U.'s
Phare program of financial aid to the struggling
economies of prospective accession countries. In
response to E.U. pressure, Polish Finance Minister
Leszek Balcerowicz implemented a series of
drastic and effective budget cuts that came to be
known as "economic shock therapy."

Later in the negotiations, the two most
contentious issues were foreign land ownership in
Poland and the right of Polish workers to look for
work in other E.U. member states. The E.U.
wanted to maintain the right of all citizens of
member states to buy land in any other member
state, as enshrined in E.U. law. Many Poles,
however, feared that this would lead to a rush of
wealthy Westerners (primarily Germans) into
Poland making offers too good for local people to
refuse. This fear is most marked in the west of
Poland, in former German lands. The real threat
of this happening seems minimal. Nevertheless,
the Polish Sejm passed a law in 1999 restricting
the sale of land to foreigners for eighteen years.

At the same time, the Polish government had
been pressing the E.U. to grant Poles the same
rights as nationals of other member states, in
particular the right to legally seek work in other
E.U. countries. Some member states, notably
Austria and Germany, feared the effects of a mass

influx of Polish workers with low wage demands taking jobs away from local workers. These fears seem as unfounded as those of the Poles regarding foreign land acquisition. For the Poles, however, the prospect of being refused the freedom to work within the E.U. after accession was akin to being stigmatized as second-class citizens.

By 2002, public support for E.U. membership had dropped close to the crucial 50 percent mark. However, the pro-Europeans prevailed, and in May 2004 Poland joined the European Union.

Andrzej Lepper: Poland's Jose Bove
If there's one person to thank for keeping the Polish evening news full of controversy, drama, and farce, it's Andrzej Lepper. His *Samoobrona* ("Self-defense") party feeds on rural discontent with foreign policy, in particular with E.U. integration. His tactics are extreme and he loves the limelight, which makes him something of a celebrity among anti-globalization groups, drawing comparisons with Jose Bove, the French activist best known for his attacks on McDonald's.

Educated urbanites may find Mr. Lepper's antics tasteless and embarrassing, but many Poles share some of his concerns regarding the E.U. It is widely believed that all that Poland represents to the E.U. is a large market in which to dump goods, and a source of cheap labor.

VALUES & ATTITUDES

Polish culture has been shaped over the centuries by many factors. The Catholic Church, great cities, Communism, generations of proud nobles, ever-shifting borders, foreign occupation, and numerous wars have all left their mark.

CATHOLICISM IN POLAND

Throughout the Communist period, the Catholic Church was the only large-scale organization outside Party control. The Church organized extra-curricular religion lessons for school children and a majority of children attended. Membership in the Church increasingly became synonymous with being against the political Establishment. This was exemplified by Pope John Paul II's first homecoming as Pope in 1979, in which more than a hundred thousand turned out for an open-air Mass in Warsaw. The Pope, a staunch anti-Communist, inspired the Solidarity Trade Union in its struggle and the trade union, in turn, became increasingly attached to conservative Catholic values.

Western European visitors to Poland may be surprised to see how strong a role the Church plays in the day-to-day lives of many Poles. Even many who do not attend Mass are strongly influenced by the culture of Polish Catholicism.

Sunday Observance
A foreigner in his first year living in Poland was quite surprised at being told off by the elderly lady in the apartment next door for using his washing machine on a Sunday. Years later, in a detached house and now safe to use the washing machine whenever he fancied, he was told off by the next door neighbor—a computer specialist in his twenties—for mowing the lawn on a Sunday!

Increasingly, however, young people are turning away from the Church as an institution, although many retain their belief. Often blamed for this disillusionment are the political ties between the Church and certain political groups. Others attribute it to the conservative values of the Polish Catholic Church and its unwillingness to change with the times. Its immovable stance on issues such as contraception and abortion, as well as the blind eye it has turned to the AIDS crisis (Poland has the highest incidence of AIDS in Central Europe), are examples of this.

It is very difficult to draw a line between religion and national culture in Poland as the two have become so intertwined. Much of the behavior that a newcomer to the country might initially attribute to strong religious belief may in fact be more an example of Polish culture. Religious celebrations are a perfect example of this. The churches are bursting at the seams, the streets are empty, and after Mass everyone rushes back to the family home for a traditional home-cooked meal washed down by a few shots of vodka. Many of those actively taking part in such traditional festivities would openly admit that they are not devout Catholics.

PRIDE AND PATRIOTISM

Poland's history has seen more than its fair share of foreign domination and war. That the Polish nation has come through this in the state it is today, a modern, relatively prosperous, Western economy, is a source of pride for Poles. However, Polish attitudes toward their state or nation are complex and may seem contradictory to many foreigners. The contradiction lies in the Polish tendency to mock their country and laugh at themselves, much as the British would, while at the same time having a straightforward, American-style pride in it. After years of mismanagement during the Communist era, the government and politicians in general remain natural objects of ridicule. But the Polish nation itself is viewed as something sacred, not to be criticized or joked about.

Thus while Poles may laugh about their plight, the state of their country, or typical Polish characteristics, foreigners should not do the same. Poles are extremely sensitive to foreign opinions of their country and themselves.

It is not at all an uncommon sight to see Polish flags flying from shop fronts and outside apartment windows on national holidays such as Constitution Day and Independence Day. Nor is it uncommon to hear the national anthem actually being sung at sporting events and official gatherings.

Local Heroes

Any Pole who gains international recognition and success is certain to be loved at home. An example of this is Adam Malysz, a young man from the mountain town of Wisla. Ski jumping was as obscure a sport in Poland as it was in most of Europe until Malysz won his first event in 1996. By the time he won the ski jumping world cup in the 2000–01 season, it had become the number-one sport in the country and Malysz was a national hero.

ATTITUDES TO RULES: IS ANYONE WATCHING?

A common stereotype of Germans is that even when driving in a forest, with no other cars for miles, they will still signal before turning. A Polish driver, on the other hand, can be in the middle of the busy city yet won't signal unless there is another car in the immediate vicinity.

In Poland, rules are not sacred—they can often be bent, or made to fit different situations. From a foreign perspective, the Polish attitude to rules can seem to be a contradictory combination of conformity and anarchy. Complex attitudes were a necessary survival technique in Communist times. Without breaking any regulations, it was almost impossible to procure sought-after goods or obtain permission for certain things that were officially banned. Other regulations, mostly political, were untouchable, however, and these were rarely tampered with. In other words, regulations were bent or broken when doing so was without consequence.

All this can have a confusing effect on foreign visitors who are unfamiliar with the "rules of the game." In the office, for example, rules that are clearly explained and whose purpose is understood are far more likely to be followed by employees than regulations that are simply stated in an impersonal manner and subsequently left unmonitored.

BRIBERY AND CORRUPTION

In the past, irksome regulations were often circumvented with a bribe. Although the daily papers are full of stories of corruption at the top levels of government and industry, such practices are increasingly becoming unacceptable. The very fact that corruption is investigated with such zeal is a positive change. Everyday corruption, or the giving of "presents," is still relatively common, but it is best for foreigners not to make such offers as the whole process is a very delicate one and offering the wrong person a bribe can cause great offense. Having said that, the line between showing gratitude and bribery can be a thin one and giving small presents to someone who has offered genuine assistance is common.

Sweeteners

A foreigner working legally in Poland was waiting rather impatiently to obtain the necessary papers from the visa office before returning home for a short visit. Frustrated at the numerous delays, he consulted a Polish colleague who suggested a box of chocolates and a bottle of brandy to show his "appreciation" to the unhelpful civil servant with whom he had been dealing. The day after delivering this present he received a telephone call telling him that his documents were ready.

CHIVALRY OR SEXISM? ATTITUDES TO WOMEN

The fact that political correctness has never really caught on in Poland can be a breath of fresh air for visitors, but at the same time certain situations can prove awkward. This is perhaps most evident in the attitudes of older Polish men toward women. On the face of it, Polish men are perfect gentlemen. Walking on the street side of the sidewalk, holding doors open, and offering seats on trams and buses are all common forms of behavior, especially among the older generation. Greetings, however, can be embarrassing for women unfamiliar or uncomfortable with having their hands kissed.

It is not at all uncommon for Polish women to have their own careers, and certain professions, such as medical doctors and lawyers, are proportionately well represented by women. However, it is much less common to see women in top management positions in large companies. A glass ceiling definitely exists in many Polish companies above which women have great difficulty progressing. Additionally, it can be difficult for a young, recently married woman to find employment in a private company owing to the employers' fear of having to pay for maternity leave. Technically it is illegal for employers to discriminate on this basis, but in reality there is almost nothing a woman can do in such a situation.

Once again the importance of the generation gap should be stressed here. Among young people attitudes to women are much more progressive and women are less likely to find themselves in awkward or difficult situations.

ATTITUDES TO MONEY

Attitudes to money differ very little between Poland and Western European countries, but there are some points to be aware of. First of all, "how much" questions should be avoided in normal conversation, whether it is in regard to someone's new computer or, of course, salaries. Many things in Poland are still cheaper than in Western Europe, a night out in particular, but try to keep to yourself your pleasure at paying $20 for a nice dinner with drinks, as most Poles consider this quite expensive.

After decades of limited opportunities to buy imported goods, many Poles now spend a large portion of their salaries on new cars, designer clothes, and electronic gadgets. In Warsaw in particular, the visitor may well be surprised by the number of luxury cars. Among businesspeople it is most unlikely that anyone in a high position would not have the appropriate class of car. Furthermore, those who own such status symbols are always eager to talk about them, while those who don't will often go into detail describing why they haven't yet got one, but plan to in the future. This is in stark contrast to rural Poland, where flashy cars, expensive clothing, or other luxury items arouse suspicion among the poor, conservative small-farming population. This class of *Nouveau riche* (a term used in Poland to refer to Russians, not themselves) illustrates the changing values in Poland and is in contrast to the malaise of the intelligentsia.

ATTITUDES TO FOREIGNERS

Much has changed in Poland in the years since Communism. One of the most visible of these changes is the influx of tourists and expatriates, especially in the large cities. The curiosity that locals used to show at a foreigner in their city has all but gone, although the sound of English in smaller towns and villages can still raise eyebrows. Foreigners can, for the most part, expect a warm welcome and kind hospitality.

As with all places, however, the warmth of the welcome may depend on where one comes from. "Westerners," especially native English speakers, are the lucky ones. First of all, English is still very popular and most young people in the cities speak a little at least. Secondly, Poles in general are fond of the English and Americans, and very curious about Canadians, Australians, and New Zealanders. In fact, during the gray days of Communist rule, Canada was synonymous with paradise in colloquial Polish.

At the opposite end of the spectrum tend to be visitors from countries of the former Soviet Union. This is largely the result of the unpleasant history between Poland and Russia, but not only. Unfortunate stereotypes abound that any "Easterner" in Poland on business must be a Mafioso or involved in some form of shady dealings. Younger people tend to be more open, however, and welcome visitors irrespective of their nationality.

Changing Attitudes

A young soccer player named Emmanuel Olisadebe from Nigeria has probably done more to combat racism in Poland than any other person or organization. After taking Polish citizenship, Olisadebe led Poland's national team in 2002 to its first World Cup appearance in over ten years. In his early days playing league soccer in Poland, hooligans threw bananas at him, but after becoming the Polish team's leading scorer, he became one of the country's best-loved celebrities.

Visitors should be prepared for many discussions about their respective views on Polish life, development, cuisine, etc. as the Poles are generally very curious about how others see them.

THE GENERATION GAP

It is a truism that values and attitudes vary from generation to generation. In the former Communist countries of Central and Eastern Europe, however, this is particularly marked. The economic changes that have taken place in Poland since 1989 have been fruitful for many but have largely left the older generation behind.

The average age of managers and directors in Poland is much younger than in Western Europe, as it is often easier for companies to train young people than to retrain those with experience in the state-run monopolies of the past. Young professionals have far more opportunities than their more experienced elders, and therefore are in a much better financial situation.

Whereas the younger generation embrace the new fashions and trends available in Poland, their parents tend to have more traditional lifestyles. Pubs, cafés, and restaurants are very popular with young, urban Poles, while the older generation prefer to entertain at home.

Educated young professionals tend to have much more open, liberal attitudes compared to the more conservative, Catholic values of their parents.

THE URBAN–RURAL GAP

While most urban centers have witnessed rejuvenation and growth in the years since the collapse of Communism, small towns and villages have suffered. The vast majority of direct foreign investment goes into the large cities, primarily Warsaw. The countryside has seen little or none of this, and those in the agricultural sector have been hardest hit by economic changes. Despite intensive urbanization during the 1940s and '50s, farming still accounts for 27 percent of Poland's workforce.

The Polish Countryside

Polish farms have traditionally been divided among siblings over the generations, resulting in increasingly numerous, but ever smaller, farms.

Flying over Germany and into Poland the change
is immediately apparent as the large tracts of land
give way to the tiny, irregular plots that make up
the Polish agricultural sector. The fact that farms
remained privately owned in Poland during
Communism seemed at the time to be a victory
for Polish farmers, but the small size of these
enterprises makes them uncompetitive when
compared with the massive, technologically
advanced agricultural sector of Western Europe.
It is estimated that half of the Polish agricultural
sector consists of subsistence farming.

THE LEGACY OF COMMUNISM

The effects of forty years of state socialism on
Polish values and attitudes are still very evident,
and not only among the generations that grew up
in the Communist system but in the younger
generation as well.

Perhaps the strongest effect has been on the
work ethic in the country. Most Poles never
really believed the socialist propaganda, and
working for the state (as the vast majority did)
increasingly became thought of as working for
an illegitimate power. As this "Us vs. Them"
atmosphere intensified, there seemed less and
less logic in doing your job well, especially with
the wasteful overemployment of the Communist

system. Stealing from the workplace was common; with the excuse "The property of the state belongs to everyone, so why not take home what is partly mine."

Another manifestation of this is in attitudes to authority. Anyone from a policeman to a train conductor who had authority over people was viewed with suspicion and elaborate systems were developed for people to "beat the system." Although this mentality is changing, negative attitudes to those in authority are still evident and foreign managers working in Poland often note the anti-authoritarian attitudes of their staff.

chapter three

CUSTOMS & FESTIVALS

Few can compete with the Poles when it comes to enthusiastic celebration. This is as true for religious and public holidays as it is for special occasions such as weddings and name days. Moreover, many Polish customs and ways of celebrating traditional Catholic holidays have a strong pagan element, giving them a unique flavor.

Throughout the decades of Communism there was little opportunity to celebrate in restaurants or pubs, and Poles became masters of entertaining at home. This also reflects the long tradition of the Polish nobility, who were famous for their hospitality and grand feasts. The Poles say "a guest in the home is God in the home," and despite the fact that Polish cities are no longer devoid of restaurants and public houses, the custom of entertaining at home is still very much alive. When invited to celebrate a holiday or special occasion with a Polish family, a foreigner is in for a treat and should be prepared for a grand feast and a late night.

PUBLIC HOLIDAYS	
January 1	New Year's Day
March/April (movable)	Easter Monday
May 1	Labor Day
May 3	Constitution Day
June (movable)	Corpus Christi
August 15	Feast of the Assumption
November 1	All Saints' Day
November 11	Independence Day
December 25	Christmas Day
December 26	Boxing Day

TRADITIONAL HOLIDAYS AND EVENTS
Carnival

Carnival in Warsaw or Krakow may not be as glamorous as in Rio de Janeiro or Venice, but it has its own charm. The first signs of Carnival are the crowds at discos and pubs. Young people in particular enjoy the carnival atmosphere as a break from the dreariness of winter, work, or upcoming exams. Those who have outgrown the disco usually organize home parties throughout the period from the New Year to the beginning of Lent—the forty days of fasting that start on Ash Wednesday and last till Easter Sunday.

In the mountains and the countryside, Poles celebrate carnival outdoors with a traditional bonfire and sleigh ride (*kulig*), while drinking plenty of mulled beer or wine to keep warm.

The last Thursday before Lent is known as Fat Thursday (*Tlusty Czwartek*). It is the day when the lines outside delicatessens and sweet shops can stretch around city blocks as the whole country gorges on traditional, sweet, heavy doughnuts (*paczki*) before, theoretically at least, having to give up such delicacies for Lent.

The climax of Carnival comes on the final three days, the so-called crazy days, before Ash Wednesday, when parties and balls are organized throughout the country. The final Tuesday of Carnival (*ostatki*) represents the last chance for strict Catholics to enjoy loud music, dancing, alcohol, meat, and sweets before the Lenten fast.

Even those who do not consider themselves religious generally respect the period of Lent, refraining from parties and avoiding conspicuous consumption. Foreigners should follow this example to avoid inadvertently causing offense.

Easter
The Easter holiday equals Christmas for tradition and importance in Poland, although Western-style consumerism in recent years has given Christmas a much glitzier appearance.

Lent culminates in "Holy Week" (*Wielki Tydzien*), beginning with Palm Sunday. Due to the lack of subtropical palms in Central Europe, Poles use pussy willows and sticks with special floral arrangements in their place. On Palm Sunday, these floral arrangements are blessed in the church, and carried through the local streets by parishioners in a procession led by the priest.

Good Friday (*Wielki Piatek*) in Poland is not a public holiday as it is in many other countries. It is, nonetheless, an important day for the faithful, and one spent in stark contrast to the joyous atmosphere of the rest of the Holy Week. Good Friday Mass is a somber occasion as worshipers reflect on the death of Christ. After Mass in many parishes a cross is carried in procession; in others there are visits to models of the Holy Sepulcher. Back at home, meanwhile, preparations will be well under way for the Easter Sunday feast.

On Holy Saturday (*Wielka Sobota*), families prepare small, elaborately decorated wicker baskets containing portions of the food to be served on Easter Sunday. Each basket, typically containing a boiled egg, piece of sausage, bread, salt, pepper, and the figure of a lamb (the symbol of Easter) made of sugar, is sprinkled with holy water and blessed by the priest after Mass.

The fasting of Lent finally ends after morning Mass on Easter Sunday, when feasting begins with a massive breakfast. In many homes the feasting continues more or less uninterrupted through the day with a variety of traditional dishes washed down with wine or vodka. The festive atmosphere, the abundance of food and drink, and the lighting of firecrackers outside are a complete contrast to the peace and quiet of Lent.

Smigus Dyngus

Those who do not like getting wet had best not visit Poland on Easter Monday, better known as *Smigus Dyngus*. In a fun tradition with clear pagan origins and connected with the coming of spring, young men roam the streets searching for victims to be drenched with water. Traditionally it was unmarried girls who were doused, but today it can be anyone with the misfortune of turning down the wrong street.

The First Week of May

The first week of May is a time to escape for a spring break as both May 1 and 3 are public holidays. May 1 is Labor Day and no longer holds any special significance in post-Communist Poland. The anniversary of the signing of Poland's first written constitution in 1791 is celebrated on May 3. Official ceremonies and parades are held and patriots fly flags from their windows, but for the most part the significance of the day is lost on the vacationing crowds. Many offices even close down altogether for the week and the cities empty as people head out in search of spring sunshine.

Corpus Christi

Those who enjoy folk costumes shouldn't miss the traditional Corpus Christi processions on the first Thursday after Trinity Sunday. The town of Lowicz, to the west of Warsaw, in particular is known for its colorful yet solemn celebrations.

All Saints' Day—All Souls' Day

The most solemn of the traditional holidays, All Saints' Day and All Souls' Day, are devoted to remembering the dead and most Poles spend these days visiting the graves of family members.

Only the first of these two days is a national holiday. The second day is dedicated to praying for the souls of the departed in the hope that they will reach heaven. Relatives of the deceased visit the cemetery, clean around the grave and, most importantly, light candles and leave flowers. The cemeteries at night have a surreal air with the warm glow from thousands of candles.

There are elements of pagan tradition mixed in with the religious devotions of All Saints' Day. There used to be, and still is to some degree, a

belief that the spirits of the dead were free to
roam on this day and food was left at the graves to
appease the spirits.

St. Andrew's Day

Another day with a mixture of Catholic and
pagan traditions is St. Andrew's Day (*Andrzejki*),
just after the fall equinox on November 30.
Although not a national holiday, many people
celebrate it by attending parties in honor of those
named Andrzej (Andrew). Children celebrate it
by, among other things, pouring melted wax
through the hole of a key into a bucket of water.
The hardened pieces of wax are then held in front
of a light, and the shadow cast against the wall is
said to predict what the coming year will bring.

St. Nicholas's Day (*Mikolajki*)

The Christmas festivities actually begin on St.
Nicholas's Day (*Mikolajki*), December 6.
Traditionally an adult would dress up in a long
robe, resembling a bishop more than the Western
Santa Claus, and distribute presents and sweets to
the good children and sticks to the naughty ones.

Christmas (*Boze Narodzenie*)

This is a very special time for Poles. In no other
holiday are national customs and traditions kept
alive as faithfully as at Christmas.

The most important day of the period is Christmas Eve (*Wigilia*). Although not an official holiday, most people either take the day off or leave work early as the festivities are meant to begin once the first star has been sighted.

The traditional *Wigilia* dinner is very specific, consisting of twelve courses, none with meat. Carp, herring, and dumplings (*pierogi*) stuffed with sauerkraut and mushrooms, and poppy seed cakes are some of the most popular dishes. An extra place is set at the table for an unexpected guest or the spirits of ancestors who are said to be present on this night. Hay is placed under a white tablecloth to represent  the stable in which Jesus was born, and pieces of hay pulled from under the tablecloth can be used to predict one's future. During the feast presents are exchanged, all supposedly from St. Nicholas. After the meal, the faithful make their way to midnight Mass, after which meat may once again be eaten.

Wigilia, like other Christian celebrations in Poland, has retained many superstitious elements that add a special flavor to the evening. Among these is the belief that animals can speak at midnight. As everyone should be at Mass, however, there is no one to hear them. Various traditional methods of fortune telling are also employed, mostly to determine the fate of any unmarried girls or predict the size of the harvest in the coming year. Many of these superstitions are remnants of pagan midwinter celebrations.

December 25 is generally spent quietly with the family. Christmas Day is the first of the twelve days of Christmas. The feasting continues on this day with *bigos*, or the traditional hunters' stew.

St. Stephen's Day (December 26) is an opportunity to visit friends and family or see the elaborate Christmas displays in churches. These may include nativity scenes, colorful castles made of tin paper, and miniature mechanized villages with moving figures, trains, etc.

New Year's Eve
New Year's Eve is yet another opportunity for a party. In Warsaw in particular, formal balls have become very fashionable with young and old alike. Entertaining at home is widespread with, in typical Polish style, a grand feast and plenty of vodka and champagne.

SPECIAL OCCASIONS
Name Days
Birthday celebrations are mostly held for children. Name days on the other hand are

celebrated in style. Practically all Poles have traditional Christian first names, and each name matches a day when that particular saint is honored. For example, anyone named Andrzej (Andrew) will celebrate his name day on St. Andrew's Day, November 30.

Unlike birthdays, there is no need for the people celebrating to tell others their age. Additionally, everyone knows by a simple glance at the calendar, when someone has their name day. The person celebrating normally organizes a small party for family and friends. A separate small celebration may be organized at work, with colleagues taking a break from their duties to sing the traditional "*Sto Lat*"— "(Live) one hundred years"—and enjoy some cake and sweets.

Weddings
Polish wedding parties are famous for their intensity and duration. Even families with limited financial resources will do all in their power to ensure that their guests are well taken care of. A typical wedding party will end the next morning, but those in the southern Tatry Mountain region are famed for lasting an entire week! In many regions of the country, including the Tatry, it is not uncommon for guests to attend the wedding in traditional folk costumes.

chapter four

MAKING FRIENDS

Poles are outgoing, gregarious, sociable people. However, on first meeting a stranger, especially without a personal introduction from a mutual acquaintance, they are often guarded and distant. They feel little need to go out of their way to be excessively polite to someone whom they know nothing about. Until very recently, such behavior was typical of shop assistants, and still is in many smaller towns and villages. Poles consider excessive politeness to strangers to be unnatural, insincere, and a little embarrassing. Such attitudes to strangers are in stark contrast with the warm welcome they reserve for friends and relatives.

MEETING THE POLES

A first-time visitor to Poland may well come to believe that, in terms of friendliness and formality, there are only two extremes. Poles seem to be either very friendly or cold and distant. In fact, the form of behavior depends on the context of the encounter. North Americans in particular, who are generally open and relatively informal with most people they meet, may find this set of social rules difficult to cope with. Americans may refer to anyone with whom they have good relations as a friend; Poles reserve this word only for those people with whom they have a very close bond, usually forged over many years.

Friends in the Right Places
Personal relationships are very important and complex in Polish society. Informal personal networks were crucial throughout the period of state socialism as it was practically impossible to do anything outside the strict regulations without "a friend in the right place." Although they are no longer a necessity, such networks have evolved and still play an important role. A Polish friend will always be happy to introduce you to a friend of theirs if it can help with a particular problem.

As personal contacts are so important in Poland, the easiest way to meet people and strike up a friendship is through a mutual friend. The fact that a third party introduces someone as a friend means that this is a person who can be trusted. Furthermore, this person will generally be accepted as a friend after such an introduction. Without such a third party, Poles can at times seem cold and suspicious when meeting someone for the first time. If you are contacting a person whose name you were given by a mutual acquaintance, be sure to mention this at the beginning of the conversation as it will make the conversation much easier.

FORMAL AND INFORMAL FORMS OF ADDRESS

Formality is a complex issue and has more to do with the relative status of individuals than it does with how they were introduced.

Hey You!

A difficult aspect of Polish conversation for foreigners is the seemingly simple distinction between "*Pan/Pani*" (Sir/Madam) and "*ty*" (you). Linguistically, such a distinction is common in many languages, but its social implications are extremely important in Poland. The bad news is that using the wrong form of address can be a *faux pas* equivalent to calling your spouse by your lover's name. The good news is that foreigners are generally excused such mistakes.

Don't be surprised when meeting with a Pole for the first time if they become awkward every time they have to use the word "you" when speaking English. On meeting someone for the first time, simple questions such as "Where do you come from" have the Polish construction "Where does Sir/Madam come from?" This very formal form of address is especially important when speaking to an elderly person, or, in business, to one's superior. This situation is normally ended when the senior person proposes they call each other by the much less formal "*ty.*"

Poles more fluent in English and more experienced in dealing with foreigners will not struggle with "you," but the social implications of this are far-reaching. Many foreign managers find that there is a huge void in Poland between formal and informal behavior. For example, it is not common at all in Poland to be on a first-name basis with one's boss. Relationships among peers may change very quickly from being extremely formal, to being the slap on the back, "best friends" variety. Americans may be comfortable with the latter, but Western Europeans tend to be used to something in between.

The best way to deal with this rather complicated situation is to say something like "Please, call me John" when constantly being referred to as Mr. Doe. Finally, make sure to address the person you are speaking to in the same way as they address you. Which means that if he's referring to you as "Mr. Smith," you may well be stuck with "Mr. Brzeszczykiewicz."

Conversation

Poles are generally easy to talk to and it is not usually difficult to strike up a conversation with a new person in a social context. Remember, however, to keep the conversation quite formal initially. Once you introduce yourself by your first name, the other person will likely do the same, after which a less formal tone may be adopted. Don't be surprised if you receive a long-winded answer to the question "How are you?" This is not used as a general greeting as it is in English-speaking countries, and is seen as an opportunity to complain about one's situation, health, or anything that comes to mind. Likewise, pleasantries such as "Have a nice day" are seen as meaningless and insincere and should be avoided. "Good-bye" ("*do widzenia*") or "see you later" ("*do zobaczenia*") are more than sufficient.

Shaking Hands, Kissing Hands, Kissing Cheeks

Another potentially awkward moment for foreigners is choosing the appropriate form of "bodily contact," both after being introduced to a Pole for the first time and when meeting again after that. These rules are also complex, but once again the generation gap is a key factor and younger Poles will be comfortable with more modern, Western greetings such as "hello" and a simple handshake.

When meeting someone for the first time or in formal situations, the standard greeting between men is "*dzien dobry*" ("good day" or "hello") followed by a firm, hearty handshake. Between women this is the standard greeting as well, but with a light handshake. In such meetings between a man and a woman unfortunately, there are no clear rules. Much here depends on the age and relative position of the two people. With younger Poles, "*dzien dobry*" and a handshake are most common, but women should be aware that older Polish men will often bow slightly to kiss a woman's hand as a sign of respect. A respectful handshake is always sufficient for a man being introduced to a Polish woman, regardless of the situation. Hand kissing is always initiated by the man and a woman will not be offended, in fact she may well be relieved, if a man does not follow this increasingly dated tradition.

In family situations, especially when seeing someone after a long absence or at holidays, Poles greet each other with a slight embrace and two or three (there is no rule here) kisses on alternate cheeks. If invited to someone's home to meet their family, be prepared for a line to form in front of you with each family member waiting to greet you in this way.

"A GUEST IN THE HOUSE IS GOD IN THE HOUSE"

This old Polish saying is still very much alive. Polish hospitality is exceptional, as is the Polish ability to throw a party. If invited to a Polish home, expect to be well taken care of; and it is not advisable to eat beforehand as a meal will probably be prepared in your honor. Even if only invited for coffee or tea, it is likely that your host will have bought some fancy cakes. Always try at least a little of what is offered. To refuse would belittle the effort taken by your host.

Meals

Be forewarned if invited for lunch, especially on a weekend, that this will be no small affair. For Poles, lunch (*obiad*) tends to be the main meal of the day. Although working hours may make this impossible for many, it is still common on weekends. Expect three or four courses made up of appetizers, soup, and one or two hot dishes, typically with meat. Homemade Polish specialities that should not be missed include dumplings stuffed with meat, cheese, or cabbage and mushroom (*pierogi*), cabbage rolls (*golabki*), and pork chops (*schabowy*).

Dinner (*kolacja*) is a smaller affair, unless guests are present. Cold appetizers, normally a selection of cheeses, cold meats, pickled herring, and salad, are eaten with bread and normally followed by a small hot dish. The star of the show here, for meat lovers at least, is the assortment of Polish sausage (*kielbasa*), which can be served hot or cold. *Kolacja*, especially in a large group, is a rather slow affair. People eat at their own pace, while washing down the food with vodka.

GIVING AND RECEIVING GIFTS

Gift giving is customary in Poland, and it is common to give something when visiting someone's home, on a first meeting, and for special occasions. Expensive gifts should be avoided except for wedding presents and other very special occasions. An expensive gift in a business context may be misunderstood as a bribe, and such gifts for normal meetings may cause embarrassment.

When visiting someone's home, a guest should always bring a token gift for the host. Some small souvenir from your own country is sufficient, as are flowers, chocolates, or a bottle of wine or spirits. Similar gifts are also appropriate for other occasions. In terms of alcohol, a bottle of spirits from your own country will be appreciated, but don't buy vodka as your host will already have prepared vodka if that's what he or she has in store for the evening.

Flowers

Polish women may well receive more flowers per capita than anywhere else in the world. Flower shops can be found on practically every street and have impressive selections. Flowers make the perfect gift for a name day or birthday, for men or women. If taken to someone's home, they should always be presented to the lady of the house.

Unlike the American tradition of buying flowers in a dozen or half dozen, flowers for social occasions should always be bought in odd numbers—even numbers are reserved for funerals. The only flowers with special significance are red roses and chrysanthemums. The former, as in Western Europe, signify romance, and the latter are traditionally bought for funerals or visiting the cemetery.

DRINKING

Poland, unfortunately, still has a huge problem with alcoholism. Evidence of this is difficult to miss, both in the cities and in the countryside. Perhaps as a reaction to this, more and more people are turning away from vodka, the traditional Polish spirit, in favor of beer and wine. In fact, wine and beer sales in Poland increased 35 percent and 34 percent respectively in 1998–2003, while sales of spirits dropped by 23 percent in the same period! At traditional gatherings, however, it is still customary to drink vodka.

Drinking Vodka

In Poland, vodka is drunk chilled (often frozen) and neat from shot glasses, with a glass of juice, mineral water, or cola close by to put out the fire. It is customary to drink in a series of toasts and not to sip at your own pace. Normally the host or most senior person proposes the toasts, but as the evening moves on, this duty may be taken up by others. If the pace is too brisk (which it usually is for foreigners), it is better to drink half a shot at a time than to miss out on a round. It is the responsibility of the host, or the person about to propose a toast, to fill the glasses of the others. Do not fill your own glass without doing so for others (there is usually no need to ask) and always fill your own glass last. Women often pass on straight vodka in favor of mixed drinks or wine, but are welcome to join in with the men if they so choose.

Drinking vodka is a serious business and, even among those who enjoy it, is increasingly reserved for special occasions, celebrations, or parties. For many, this means every Saturday night! In pubs and restaurants, however, there is very little difference in the drinking habits of Poles and those of Western Europeans.

chapter **five**

AT HOME

Because Poles go out less often than many other Europeans, the home is not just a residence, but a social meeting place where the door is always open to friends and family.

THE POLISH FAMILY
The family is central to Polish culture. Different generations of the same family keep in regular contact and a great many Poles make a weekly migration to their family home for the weekend.

Children
The statistically average Polish family has 1.5 children, a rate very similar to those of Western European countries, despite the strong objections of the Catholic Church to contraception. This rate
is dropping, however, as the demands of the new free-market economy leave people with less time to spend with their families.

Foreigners may find the degree to which parents and grandparents pamper their children excessive. It is unheard of to take a child out in any season but summer without first bundling the little one up in layers of clothing, hats, mittens, etc. Foreigners who fail to do the same with their own children will meet with the disapproving gaze and comments of nearly every *babcia* (grandmother) they come across. A similar attitude prevails when it comes to finding day care or a school for a child. Great care is taken that the school meets the parents' rigorous standards, and distance has little bearing in this decision.

This very protective attitude usually lasts till the child is a young teenager, after which parents give their children much greater freedom. It is common, for example, for groups of teenagers to take vacations together without adult supervision.

Poles have the status of minors until their eighteenth birthday, after which they enjoy such freedoms as the right to vote, and, more clearly evident, the right to drink legally. Many pubs and clubs, especially in the cities, are full of eighteen- to twenty-year-olds, as well as younger teens taking advantage of the generally relaxed attitude to underage drinking.

Senior Citizens

It is quite common for retired people to live with
their married children, to help in the house and
with the grandchildren. Such a situation serves a
dual purpose since most senior citizens require
financial assistance from their children, as the
government pension of approximately $150 a
month is insufficient to support a normal life.
Nursing homes are practically unheard of, and
people without family members to help them out
financially or with accommodation find it very
difficult to make ends meet. The elderly are
respected in Polish society. Poles will often give up
their place in a line or their seat in a bus, tram, or
train to an elderly person.

THE POLISH HOME

A large percentage of Poles live in apartment
blocks, although detached houses and luxury
condominiums are rapidly increasing in
popularity. The housing boom in Warsaw, which
started in the early 1990s, is still going strong as
those with the necessary means escape the dreary
council housing, regarded as a bad hangover from
the 1970s and 1980s. Due perhaps to this
hangover, there is a "the bigger the better" attitude
to housing. Throughout the country, huge, often
tacky, new villas can be seen next to small,

wooden shacks. There is little homogeneity to housing, either in terms of size or style, with the exception of new, Western-style housing developments built on the outskirts of large cities.

It is typical in Poland to give far more attention to the interior design of a home than to its external appearance. Even blocks that may look like slums from the outside are unrecognizable once you go inside. Apartments are normally owned, not rented, and the owners will spend years and a large portion of their income in making their homes as comfortable as possible.

RENTING AN APARTMENT

Apartments are rented directly from the individual owner. The best way to go about this, especially for a foreigner, is to use an agency. Ask a friend if they can recommend a good one, but even without such a recommendation, agents are generally honest and trustworthy. The standard agent's fee is 50 percent of one month's rent. An alternative to agents is to look in the classified ads section (*drobne ogloszenia*) of a local newspaper with the help of a Polish speaker. About half of the telephone numbers in ads you find, however, will be numbers of estate agents and not the individual owner.

An unfurnished apartment typically comes with electrical fixtures and basic kitchen and bathroom cupboards. An apartment listed as furnished could mean anything from fully furnished to a bed, table, and chair. Be forewarned that many apartments for rent will be furnished with very old, worn-out items.

It is also worth noting that smaller hotels have reasonable rates for monthly room rental, sometimes with a kitchenette included.

APPLIANCES
In smaller apartments, a small washing machine is usually kept in a corner of the kitchen or bathroom. Clothes dryers and dishwashers are somewhat of a luxury and normally found only in large houses. Outlets in Poland are the standard two-prong, 220-volt European standard, and adapters for small American appliances are readily available in hardware or electronics shops.

Low-Tech/High-Tech
The washing machine may be old and the dishwasher nonexistent, but a Polish home without the latest television and stereo system is difficult to find. Perhaps because of the years when such luxuries could only be dreamed of,

many Poles will not hesitate to spend the equivalent of two months' salary on a new television. The ease with which credit can be arranged in all medium- to large-size shops and supermarkets has fueled this consumption.

When not working, Poles tend to watch a lot of television by European standards, although much less than Americans. It is not unusual for the television to be left on even when someone is entertaining. Guests may find themselves seated around the table, enjoying a meal while watching the news, a film, or a sporting event.

EVERYDAY SHOPPING

Supermarkets exist in abundance and have become part of everyday life. Many Poles buy their nonperishable goods at Western-type supermarkets while preferring to buy fresh produce at the market. American-style shopping malls have also sprouted up in recent years and are proving to be extremely popular, especially during the long Polish winter when strolling down the high street isn't so pleasant.

Corner shops are everywhere, even in the smallest village, and often carry everything from fresh produce and meat to a range of spirits. Such shops are at the heart of the local community and are popular places for locals to meet and gossip.

Beware, however, especially at night, of men
standing outside the shop drinking beer. They are
not dangerous but can be difficult to shake off.

WORK

Only a tiny minority of Poles have gone through
the transition from state socialism to a free-
market economy without experiencing massive
changes in their lives. To begin with, under the
socialist system there was full employment, which
resulted in overemployment, that is, too many
people to do too little work. This, coupled with
the increasingly negative attitudes toward the state
in the 1980s, resulted in an abysmal work ethic.
The upside of this was that the working days were
short, typically 8:00 a.m. to 3:00 p.m., and
families spent a great deal of time together.

The contrast between then and now is extreme.
Despite the high profile of trade unions in
Poland, most workers have very few rights, and
office workers in particular are often expected to
work ten-hour days with no additional overtime
payment. With no minimum wage in effect, many
Poles hold down two jobs in order to get by.

Unemployment

Approximately 20 percent of Poland's workforce
is unemployed and would consider those with two

jobs to be the lucky ones. This figure can be deceptive, however, as much of the workforce works "in the gray," as Poles say. High employer contributions and bureaucracy force many small companies to hire employees in this way. Additionally, Poles have a great entrepreneurial spirit and many of the unemployed and retired people are involved in some sort of small business to help make ends meet.

EDUCATION

On the face of it, the education system in Poland is a success. The country has one of the world's highest adult literacy rates at 99 percent. In recent years, however, there has been much discussion in the press regarding the level of literacy among

adults, especially those living in small villages in the countryside. It has been estimated that one-third of adults have difficulty understanding what is written in a standard daily newspaper.

Sweeping reforms to the state education system introduced in the 1998–99 school year targeted deficiencies in the old system, largely unchanged since Communist times. The reforms, however, did not address the key problem of teachers' pay. With salaries lower than $500 per month, many competent teachers have left the profession and young people are reluctant to consider education as a career.

Under the current system, preschool education (*zerowka*) is compulsory from the age of six. From seven to thirteen years of age children attend primary school, after which they enter *gimnazjum*, or junior secondary school, where they spend three years. Secondary school (*liceum*) is a further three years (ages sixteen to nineteen), and pupils can choose between an academic school preparing them for university entry or a technical school that prepares them for employment as a skilled worker. Pupils normally graduate from secondary school at nineteen years of age.

University enrollment has increased greatly in recent years as has the number of those entering postgraduate studies. The current economic climate provides few opportunities for those without a university education.

THE CITY AND THE COUNTRYSIDE

Once again, the difference between the lifestyles of those living in large cities and those in the countryside must be stressed. City dwellers tend to work longer hours, have a superior financial position, and lead much less traditional lives than their rural compatriots. The fast pace of Warsaw in particular is a far cry from life in the country.

One needs only to travel twenty miles from the city to see the contrast. In the countryside it is common to see villagers, elderly women in particular, sitting on benches outside their homes, next to the street watching the world go by. Elderly men still tip their hats when they wish "*dzien dobry*" ("Good day") to passersby and spend hours outside the village shop chatting with other locals.

Country Ways

Two foreigners were walking through a small village on a sunny day when the heavens opened and they took refuge under the eaves of an old barn next to a run-down farmhouse. After some minutes the front door opened and a man motioned for them to come in. Surprised that his guests didn't speak Polish, the farmer summoned his daughter to translate. He welcomed them to his home and prepared a table of bread, butter, cheese, and ham. The customary bottle of vodka appeared and for the next three hours the group ate, drank, and exchanged stories. When it was time to move on, the daughter produced a bag full of homemade cheeses and ham for the departing guests.

chapter six

TIME OUT

Among the positive changes that have come about
since the end of Communism has been the
exponential growth in possibilities for spending free
time. Cinemas, theaters, pubs, clubs, restaurants,
shopping malls, and recreation centers are all
available to Poles today. Despite this profusion of
modern alternatives, the traditional Polish passion
for the great outdoors is undiminished.

During long weekends and holidays in particular
the cities empty and their inhabitants head *en masse*
for the seaside, lakes, mountains, or family homes in
the countryside. Although the Poles work long
hours, they have generous vacation breaks and few
would even contemplate spending their free days at
home. Foreign vacations have also become extremely
popular as the prices have dropped to destinations
such as Southern Europe, North Africa, and the Alps.

EATING OUT

It wasn't long ago that even in large cities there
were only two possibilities available to diners.

There were cheap bars offering little more than greasy cutlets, boiled potatoes, and sauerkraut. In fact in the 1980s even that would have been a lucky find! At the other extreme were posh, very expensive restaurants, although the food and service rarely lived up to the prices.

Today, however, thanks largely to greatly increased competition in cities and large towns, a wealth of possibilities exists for those in search of an interesting dining experience at a very reasonable price.

It is not common for restaurants to display their menus outside or in the window, but it is perfectly acceptable to enter and ask to see the *karta* (menu). In restaurants and cafés it is common to find an English translation of the menu, although this can often be as difficult to understand as the Polish version! "*Bars*"—cheap cafeterias—are usually self-service and you'll be hard pressed to find either an English menu or an employee who can translate.

If you are a vegetarian, remember that vegetarianism is not yet as common in Poland as in many other countries. It is not a bad idea therefore to check whether there are vegetarian dishes available when choosing a restaurant. If someone else is choosing, make them aware of your dietary needs. It is not at all frowned upon to decline meat dishes, although you will almost certainly be in the minority.

Smokers coming from countries where their right to light up is severely restricted will find Poland a welcome retreat. Those who are put off by cigarette smoke, however, will have a difficult time finding a restaurant or café with a non-smoking section worthy of the name. Under Polish law, such areas must be provided in every establishment, but nonsmokers are often placed in a back corner only a few feet away from the ubiquitous cigarette smoke of others.

Ethnic Cuisine
While the range of ethnic restaurants in Polish cities may be limited, Italian, Chinese, Turkish, and Greek cuisine are all well represented. North African and Balkan cafés and restaurants are also well worth seeking out.

Polish Cuisine
As for Polish cuisine, it is not as easy as one would think to sample local specialities prepared to the same standard as foreign dishes. Polish food is regarded (and rightfully so) as being best prepared at home. Try a Polish dish in a restaurant and it is very likely that your Polish colleague will comment that their mother or grandmother prepares it in a different and superior way.

There are, however, restaurants that do as much credit to Polish cuisine as anyone's mother or grandmother. Ask a Polish acquaintance to recommend a place and, if possible, to join you to help you work through the menu.

Polish specialities well worth trying include *zurek* (a creamy, sour soup with sausage and boiled egg), *golabki* (stuffed cabbage rolls), *placki* (potato pancakes), *bigos* (traditional stew), and *pierogi* (dumplings, usually stuffed with meat, cabbage, or white cheese).

Coffee and Tea

If vodka is Poland's national drink, then tea must be the second. Tea is drunk in huge quantities by both young and old, and it is normally taken with a slice of lemon and no milk. In fact, you may receive strange looks when asking for milk for your tea as it is normally only pregnant and breast-feeding women who drink it this way.

Coffee has become increasingly popular in recent years, although the serving method may cause coffee aficionados to cringe. For years when coffee was hard to come by and coffeemakers were virtually unheard of, Poles made what was erroneously referred to as "Turkish coffee" (*kawa po Turecku*). This involves putting a spoonful or two of regular ground coffee into a cup then adding boiling water and stirring. Fortunately the only place you may inadvertently be served "Turkish coffee" these days is in one of the cheapest bars. Beware when taking that last sip or you may end up with coffee grounds in your teeth! At home, however, many Poles still prepare their coffee this way, although instant is also very popular. Most cafés and restaurants today serve coffee from espresso machines. American-style drip-filtered coffee is virtually nonexistent.

Drinks

As we have seen, vodka is widely drunk at home on special occasions, or at parties. In restaurants, pubs, and cafés it is generally only drunk by groups of people (usually men) celebrating. It is not a casual drink and as such is less popular than beer and wine when Poles go out. Beer, in fact, has become very popular in recent years with both men and women, of all ages and social classes. It is certainly the drink of choice for young Poles.

Polish beers are very good. Lagers are most common, with leading brands named after regions or towns such as Zywiec, Tyskie, and Okocim.

Wine is also increasing in popularity, although Poland is not a wine-producing country. Reasonably priced quality wines from the Balkans can be found in most shops and restaurants.

WHERE TO DRINK

The Polish word "*bar*" does not mean a place to drink, but rather a cheap, simple place to get a bite to eat; something between a cafeteria and a café. It may or may not be licensed to serve alcohol.

A "*drink bar*," on the other hand, is a place for drinking, often of a serious nature. Such places are best avoided by foreigners as they tend to be cheap hangouts for local drunks or, in the cities, inhabited by "working women" and their bosses.

To wet your whistle, it is best to find a pub or a café where the atmosphere is usually cosy and quiet. Cafés close relatively early, whereas pubs generally close at 11:00 p.m., but may well remain open till sunrise.

Service

Despite horror stories from the 1980s and early 1990s about the standards of service in Poland (all of them true!), today's reality is greatly different. In large cities, with the exception of cheap bars or drink bars, standards are very similar to most Western European countries. However, you may just occasionally experience the rudeness and reluctance of Communist-era service. This can happen in restaurants of every type.

TIPPING

Rules regarding tipping are not written in stone and many diners do not leave anything. Because of this perhaps, tips are very much appreciated by the staff. Generally speaking, if the service is satisfactory a 10 percent tip is appropriate.

Do not say "thank you" when paying your bill unless you intend to leave the change as a tip! "Thank you" ("*dziekuje*") is a euphemism for "keep the change" when paying a bill. This is why your thanks when paying a bill will always be greeted with a broad smile.

NIGHTLIFE

The nighttime scene varies greatly from city to city, with virtually nothing happening in smaller towns. The old town square in Krakow is abuzz with pub hoppers till the wee hours, while in the industrial city of Katowice it can be a challenge to find anything open after 10:00 p.m. Generally speaking, however, Polish pubs have no strict regulations regarding last call, and many advertise themselves as staying open "till the last guest." It's usually not difficult to find a place open till 1:00 or 2:00 a.m. in Warsaw or Krakow.

As for nightclubs and discos, there's no point showing up before 11:00 p.m. as nothing much will be happening. The action starts between 11:00 p.m. and midnight and usually lasts till around 3:00 a.m. Practically all nightclubs charge an entrance fee, usually 20 or 30 zloty. Poles, young and old, love to dance, so put on your dancing shoes!

Safety

Poland is not a particularly dangerous country, although the change from being an extremely safe country during Communist times to becoming a country with normal, Western-style dangers has shocked many older Poles. It is advisable to take a taxi at night rather than walk, and to beware of pickpockets in crowded places. Finally, in drinking establishments, be wary of "friends" who become interested in you once they hear you speaking a foreign language. Such characters are normally harmless drunks but it's best to apologize, make up an excuse, and move on.

TOURIST SHOPPING

Shopping in large Polish cities differs little from elsewhere in Europe. One can find high-quality, high-priced boutiques and specialty shops in the center or old town intermixed with cafés, delicatessens, and souvenir shops.

Polish markets are worth experiencing, whether it's the flower markets, farmers' markets, or those to be found in larger cities with traders, mostly from the former Soviet Union, selling anything under the sun. If possible, ask a Polish friend or colleague to recommend a good market and to accompany you as it will be difficult to cope without a translator. It is worth noting that market traders rarely haggle and the price you see is probably what you'll have to pay, although no offense will be taken if you try.

Shopping hours in Poland are quite generous by European standards. Main street shops are typically open from 10:00 a.m. till 7:00 p.m. Monday to Friday, and Saturday from 9:00 a.m. to 2:00 p.m. Although there are no legal restrictions on Sunday shopping, most small shops are closed, with the exception of the odd convenience store or pharmacy. Shopping centers and supermarkets are usually open from 10:00 a.m. till 9:00 p.m. Monday through Saturday, and varying hours on Sundays.

Souvenirs

Among the more popular purchases for foreigners
in Poland are amber, silver, crystal, vodka, pottery,
and handmade craft items. Although all of these
items are cheaper in Poland than in most other
European countries, be aware that prices in tourist
areas such as old town squares and hotel gift shops
will be considerably higher than elsewhere.

MONEY

Although Poland is a member of the European
Union, it does not use the single currency. The
Polish zloty (PLN) is the country's currency and
one zloty is made up of 100 groszy. Banknotes are
in denominations of 10, 20, 50, 100, and 200 zloty.

All major Western currencies are easily
exchanged in any city at banks, hotels, or
exchange kiosks, called *kantor* in Polish. It is
worth changing your money in a *kantor* as they
are perfectly safe and trustworthy, with better
exchange rates than banks and hotels. Different
kantors will have slightly different rates, so it may
be worth comparing a few if exchanging a

large sum. The rate
displayed outside the
kantor is the actual
rate with no additional
fees or charges.

Travelers' checks should be cashed at your hotel or in a bank, as they are not normally accepted in shops. Visa and Eurocard/Mastercard are accepted in most large shops and restaurants, as are bank cards compatible with the Euronet network. Bank machines are easy to find and are most commonly located in shopping centers, gas stations, supermarkets, shopping streets, and tourist areas, as well as in any bank.

Since personal checks are not used in Poland, personal or large financial transactions are normally settled by bank transfer. A Polish bank account, therefore, may prove useful for anyone staying for an extended period of time. Bank accounts are easy to open for foreigners and require only standard documents.

Poland hasn't experienced rampant inflation since the early 1990s and is unlikely to experience it again any time soon. In fact, many prices in the tourist sector such as hotels and flights have fallen in recent years.

STAGE AND SCREEN
Polish Theater

The theater as an institution has played a special role in Polish culture. Throughout the period of political censorship under the Communist regime many playwrights managed to outsmart the censors and slide derogatory references to the system into their plays. Today the theater remains popular with young and old alike, whether it's traditional, experimental, or modern. Many theater companies have won international acclaim and all Polish cities have a number of theaters to choose from. A must for lovers of experimental theater is the Witkiewicz

Theater in the historic mountain resort town of Zakopane. It is well worth the trip, despite the fact that the repertoire is entirely in Polish.

One form of theater that illustrates the paradox of Polish culture in a very specific way is cabaret. This is something between the Western form of song-and-dance cabaret and satire. It can be found in any size of venue, from small restaurants to the largest theaters, and is a favorite on Polish television. No politician or celebrity is safe from the barbs of those on stage. More often parodied than any individuals, however, is Poland itself, or perhaps more accurately, Polishness. The various cabarets manage to walk the paradoxical line of showing pride in the country while making fun of it at the same time.

Opera and Ballet

In the years of Communism, factory workers and miners were taken for nights out to the opera or ballet in an attempt to make high culture available to the masses. Although the experiment had limited success, one positive element remains, and that is the ticket prices. Polish opera and ballet companies are of a high standard, and are still subsidized, with ticket prices that actually do make high culture accessible to all. International and Polish composers feature in the repertoire of most companies. Many Polish cities have their own ballet and opera but Warsaw's Grand Theater (Teatr Wielki), one of Europe's largest theaters, is the venue of choice.

Cinema
Going to the movies is very popular in the cities, especially among the young. There is no shortage of cinemas, including modern multiplex facilities, often located in shopping centers. The good news for visitors in the mood for a film is that foreign-language films are shown with their original soundtracks with Polish subtitles. Smaller towns rarely have facilities to match those in the cities and the price of tickets is prohibitive for many.

Poland is well known internationally for its acclaimed directors. Among these are Roman Polanski, Andrzej Wajda, and the late Krzysztof Kieslowski.

OUTDOOR ACTIVITIES

The Poles have a great love for the outdoors, and while this may not be evident on a winter's day in Warsaw, take a trip to one of the country's many national or regional parks on a sunny day to see for yourself. Poland has much to offer both summer and winter sports enthusiasts.

Walking and Hiking

Walking and hiking are favorite pastimes. Trails are well-marked, and there are clear, concise, tourist site maps. Destinations for walking and hiking vacations are the national parks and various historical sites. The Bialowieza National Park to the east of the country on the Belorussian border has the largest original lowland forest in Europe and is a paradise for those who love walking in the woods.

The Tatry, Sudety, Pieniny, and Bieszczady Mountains, all in the south of the country, offer excellent hiking with a well-developed tourist infrastructure, including a wide range of accommodation to choose from. It is customary to wish "good  day" ("*dzien dobry*") to fellow hikers whom you pass in the mountains.

Cycling

Recreational cycling has greatly increased in recent years, despite the fact that biking paths are virtually nonexistent. If you plan on cycling be aware that motorists will pay little heed to you and this can be an alarming experience. In the countryside, bicycles are still used more as a practical means of transportation than a form of recreation.

Be extremely careful to lock your bike any time it is left unattended. Bicycle theft is big business in Poland.

Skiing

All the mountain ranges to the south of the country offer alpine skiing facilities. The Tatry Mountains, being the highest, generally have the best conditions and most reliable snow. The quality of lifts and snow grooming equipment can be disappointing, however, for those used to skiing in Western European resorts, as can the long lines for the lifts.

Sailing

The Mazury Lakes sixty miles northeast of Warsaw is the place to go for sailing. On a hot summer's day the lakes and lakeshore beer gardens come alive with sailing enthusiasts. It is possible to rent a boat with or without a crew.

The Baltic also provides opportunities for sailing, but the winds, waves, and unpredictable weather make it less popular than the lakes for weekend sailors.

TRAVELING

Getting from A to B in Poland can be a trying experience, depending on your destination. The good news is that traveling between major cities is quick, reliable, and inexpensive. The bad news is that if your destination is a little off the beaten track, there may be no good news, except for an interesting cultural experience. Transportation links are constantly improving, however, as more money flows into the infrastructure.

ENTERING POLAND
If flying to Poland, you will most likely arrive either in Warsaw or Krakow, although international flights are also available to Bydogoszcz, Katowice, Poznan, Szczecin, and Wroclaw. There are many direct rail links to Berlin, Prague, Budapest, and Vienna.

Visas
With Poland's entry to the European Union, the entry requirements have undergone many

changes and these changes are continuing. Please
verify any of the information given
below with your local Polish consulate.
For visits of up to ninety days'
duration, no visa is required for
citizens of the U.S.A. and E.U. member
states, including other new accession states.

Passport Control and Customs
Generally speaking, this is a straightforward
matter, no different from that in Western E.U.
member states. Currency declarations are a thing
of the past as are intrusive customs inspections.
European travelers will have an easier time of it
than those from outside the E.U., who may be
held up at passport control.

GETTING AROUND
By Rail
There are four standards of train (*pociag*)
in Poland: InterCity/EuroCity, express
(*ekspresowy*), fast train (*pospieszny*), and
commuter train (*osobowy*).

InterCity and EuroCity trains travel between
major cities, usually nonstop, with the latter
servicing certain international routes. As well as
being a fast, efficient means of transportation,
these trains are very comfortable and have

complimentary tea or coffee and a restaurant car.
Reservations are required both for first and
second class.

Express trains cover more routes than the
InterCity service and are equally fast, but with
older carriages, no complimentary coffee and tea,
and a self-service bar car. Reservations are
compulsory for both classes on express trains.

Fast trains travel similar routes to the
InterCity and Express services but with many
more stops. The standard of
the carriages may be
considerably lower and there
may or may not be a bar car.
Reservations on fast trains are
optional, but recommended, especially on busy
routes at peak hours.

Commuter trains are best avoided. The trains
are old and worn out, overcrowded, and can be
havens for pickpockets. There average speed is
about 20 mph (32 kmph) and they stop at just
about every village on the way, even if the village
consists of three houses, eight people, and twelve
cows. If you must reach a small town or village
and are without a car this, unfortunately, may be
your only choice.

Tickets for all trains can be purchased at the
station, at a travel agent (look for Orbis, the state
travel agency), or from a conductor on board with

a small surcharge. Be careful with your bags on trains, especially when traveling at night and on international routes. Sleeping passengers all too often fall prey to stealthy thieves wandering the corridors.

It is common for passengers entering a compartment to wish "Good day" ("*dzien dobry*") to each other upon entering and "Good-bye" ("*do widzenia*") when leaving. In case you haven't got a reserved seat, it's polite to ask if a seat is free (*wolne*) before claiming it.

By Car

For reaching locations other than city centers, traveling by car is the most convenient option. It is a big advantage, however, if you have a Polish colleague to drive you, as Polish roads and motorists can make driving a challenge. The state of the roads is one of the most visible signs that Poland still lags behind the E.U.'s Western member states in economic development. Polish drivers can be very aggressive and will think nothing of cruising along at 60 mph (97 kmph) or more on a narrow road, swerving to avoid the potholes that make an obstacle course out of many of the country's roads.

To drive in Poland, holders of a European driver's license do not require any other documents. In addition to a valid driver's license, those without a European license will need to obtain an international driver's permit from their automobile association before leaving for Poland.

Road signs and markings are of the standard European type, so non-European drivers should consult a driver's guide to make sense of it all. Finally, beware of tram lines in cities. Trams have the right of way in all situations.

By Bus

Traveling by bus in Poland can be anything from a quick, comfortable, air-conditioned journey to an endurance test involving standing in an overcrowded bus bouncing over bumpy roads and either sweltering in the heat or freezing to death, depending on the season. It's unlikely you'll end up on the latter by mistake, but by purchasing your ticket at the state tourist agency (Orbis) or a private travel agent, you should safely avoid a shocking cultural experience.

On the other hand, traveling to Poland from Western Europe by bus is predictably comfortable, as only newer, high standard vehicles are licensed to drive these routes. It is usually only marginally slower than going by train and can be considerably cheaper. The bus tends to be the transportation of choice for Polish students on vacation.

By Plane

Flying between Polish cities has become considerably cheaper in recent years, especially at weekend rates. The only problem is that for many routes, Warsaw to Krakow for example, by the time you get to the airport, wait to board, and take a taxi after arriving at your destination, you may as well have saved money by taking the train. From the center of Warsaw to the center of Krakow takes 2.5 hours by express or InterCity train. This would be hard to beat by plane as an hour would probably be spent getting to and from the airports. A local travel agent will help you to plan the best method of getting where you want to go.

LOCAL TRANSPORTATION

Public Transportation

The standard of public transportation varies greatly depending where in the country you are. In larger cities, however, the service is quite efficient and very affordable. Virtually all major cities have two main forms of public  transportation: tram and bus. The old Communist-era trams and buses are slowly being removed from service, but many remain. Trams are a better bet if you are in a rush as they avoid most of the jams.

Both trams and buses run regularly from approximately 5:00 a.m. to 11:00 p.m., Monday to Saturday, with reduced service on Sundays and public holidays. In large cities on weekdays you shouldn't have to wait for a tram or bus for more than ten minutes. Warsaw has the country's only subway service (*metro*), but it consists of only one line that runs to the residential district of Ursynow.

Each city has its own transit tickets and they are valid for all forms of public transportation within that city. Kiosks, normally located on all main streets, are the places to buy a ticket (*bilet*). Failing that, in most cities it is possible to buy a ticket from the tram or bus driver, although the cost is marginally higher. After boarding the tram or bus your ticket must be validated in one of the ticket punch machines. If unsure what to do, take your cue from the other passengers. If in town for a long stint, weekly and monthly tickets are also available at the kiosks or any post office. Tickets are checked randomly by "undercover" ticket inspectors. Fines for traveling without a ticket are the only thing that is not cheap about public transportation, so don't take any chances.

Taxis

Taxis are a fast, efficient, and cost-effective way of getting around in Polish cities. There is certainly no shortage of taxis in large cities and you shouldn't have to wait long to find a vacant one. There are, however, some things to be aware of.

First of all, taxi drivers are generally very honest and will rarely take advantage of foreigners. This is not the case at airports and train stations, however. Never take a ride with a cabbie loitering in the arrivals area asking if you need a taxi, or you will almost certainly be taken for a ride in more ways than one. Check for a taxi information desk in the arrivals area of the airport. The people there will arrange a proper cab for you with standard rates. This system works very well at Warsaw International Airport.

Not many taxi drivers will speak English, so if your Polish skills are weak or nonexistent it's a good idea to write down your destination on a piece of paper that you can then show to the driver.

Never take a taxi without a company name and phone number clearly marked on it. If there is simply a rooftop sign bearing the word "Taxi," look for another. Phoning for a taxi is always a good idea. Waiters, waitresses, office and hotel receptionists will always be happy to call a cab for you.

By law, fares must be displayed in the window. Note, however, that there are higher tariffs at night, on Sundays, and holidays and for trips outside the city limits. Tipping is not very common, but rounding up the fare will always be appreciated.

WHERE TO STAY

Accommodation in Poland comes in all shapes and sizes. Whatever type you choose, however, the standards of safety and hygiene are generally high.

While all hotels in Poland use the same five-star rating system as most European countries, this works only as a general guide and can be rather inconsistent. For the sake of comparison, types of accommodation will be covered in three categories: high-end, medium-priced, and budget.

All cities have free information guides in English that can be found at airports, train stations, tourist information centers, and Orbis tourist centers. Use these to help find an appropriate hotel for your needs.

High-end Accommodation

Unfortunately, accommodation is not one of the things that Western visitors will find inexpensive in Poland. In fact, the very opposite may be the case, especially when it comes to international hotels in Warsaw. For many years there was a lack of high-standard hotels in Polish cities, resulting in high prices and low vacancy rates in those that could be found. The situation is improving in terms of vacancies, but prices remain high. Together with the Western prices, however, come Western standards.

In addition to Western hotel chains, there are many top-class Polish hotels where you can experience a little more Polish culture. If you have time to visit a resort such as Sopot on the Baltic coast, or Zakopane in the Tatry Mountains, and if your budget allows, a few nights in such a hotel is well worth the investment.

Medium-priced Accommodation

Searching out a hotel in this category, you are certain to come across many Orbis hotels. Throughout the Communist era, Orbis was the state tourist organization and controlled most of the country's hotels. Today, Orbis runs a collection of prewar, Communist-era, and modern hotels. These tend to be in the medium to high price range, conveniently located, and well equipped with restaurants, cafés, bars, etc. Even if the hotel's exterior is a reminder of the drab, socialist architecture of the 1970s, the interior may well be pleasant and modern.

Besides Orbis, there is a vast choice of smaller, privately owned hotels in this price range. They are often friendlier and cosier than the larger hotels, and more likely to be located in the old quarters, but can also be disappointing. Ask a friend or colleague if they can recommend a good hotel or visit a tourist information center.

At the lower end of this price range are pensions (*pensjonat*). Mostly found in smaller towns and tourist resorts, they are often rich in character and located in old buildings. Breakfast is usually included in the price and full board can often be arranged as well.

Budget Accommodation

Much of the accommodation available in this category is workers' hostels. State companies, trade unions, and students' organizations often own vacation homes in tourist areas and small hostels in cities that are intended for the use of their members. FWP is one of the largest such organizations. Extra rooms are rented out, however, and there are some good deals to be found. The rooms are typically basic but spotlessly clean, normally with a toilet and

sometimes a shower. If not, there is usually a communal shower on every floor. If you choose this option, make sure to inquire about a curfew. The doors are often locked at 11:00 p.m. or midnight, although there is usually a doorbell to wake the slumbering attendant to let you in.

Typical student hostels exist in large cities, but are not abundant in Poland. As such, they tend to be overcrowded and there are often no free places available. Curfews may be strictly enforced, so beware!

Finally, private accommodation is a popular choice with many Poles traveling on a budget. In resort areas you may be met at the train or bus station by people trying to convince you to come stay at their place. If you go with them, make it clear beforehand that you just want to have a look and don't commit unless you're satisfied with the place and a price has been agreed on. A better solution is to check if there is a local tourist office that will arrange private accommodation for you. Note that this is not the equivalent of an English-style bed and breakfast. It is typically just a room with shared bathroom and kitchen facilities. Don't expect your hosts to go out of their way for you because they probably won't.

chapter eight

BUSINESS BRIEFING

Many of the Western expatriates living in Poland have come to the country on business. Until recently a large percentage of the top managers and directors of Western companies operating in Poland were themselves Westerners, but this has begun to change and today experienced, qualified Poles are more likely to be found in such positions. Many Polish managers and directors therefore have already had substantial contact with Western businesspeople and are familiar with general Western business etiquette, negotiation techniques, etc. This puts them in an advantageous position when doing business with a foreigner who has little or no idea about how Poles conduct business. Having at least a basic understanding of how to do business with Poles therefore is crucial for success.

At first glance, Polish business culture seems to be a hodgepodge of old socialist-era networks, hard-selling, fast-talking American sales techniques, and everything in between. While

there may, in fact, be some truth to this,
an unwritten code of conduct exists. Some of
these unwritten rules are general and others are
specific to particular groups.

POLISH BUSINESSPEOPLE

The people you may be doing business with in
Poland could be young, educated managers, fluent
in English and with a very familiar business style.
On the other hand, you may well meet with senior
managers whose experience comes from running
elephantine socialist state corporations.

The Old Guard

Although steadily decreasing in number, many of
today's Polish managers are still former directors
of state companies from the 1970s and 1980s.
First of all, don't jump to the conclusion that they
are old Communist dinosaurs with no idea how
to work in a modern business environment.
Although there is no shortage of such examples to
be found, many managers with experience from
the former system are as skilled at making their
way in today's reality as they were in yesterday's.
Furthermore, they often have contacts in the right
places, which is crucial in Polish business.

When meeting with such people it is good to
remain more formal than you would with

younger business contacts. Choose a classy restaurant if inviting them out, and don't refer to them by their first names unless invited to do so.

Such contacts can offer valuable insights into the inner workings of Polish business. They understand the changes, past and present, facing the business community and tend to have a wealth of contacts that can help them in a range of situations. This is particularly useful in dealing with the miles of red tape needed to do business in Poland.

Red tape frustrates both Poles and foreigners alike. In fact the various regulations are often contradictory and seemingly change on a daily basis. This is especially true when it comes to tax regulations. Many Poles hoped that European Union integration would solve such problems, as Polish regulations had to come into line with those of the E.U. The result in many cases, however, has been a duplication of paperwork. To further complicate the matter, many Polish regulations are not spelled out clearly, leaving much room for "interpretation" on the part of government officials who must give their approval. This has led to further opportunities for corruption among civil servants.

The New Guard
With MBA and other business programs at Polish universities oversubscribed, and with

unemployment in Poland at postwar highs, there is a surplus of young, well-educated junior managers. The key for them is experience, and those who have managed to combine their studies with the right professional work experience will have no shortage of opportunities. What they may lack in terms of international experience, they make up for in effort and determination. It is not uncommon for young Polish managers to work between ten to twelve hours per day.

What these young professionals may lack, however, is the perspective of the older generation. Things do not change overnight, and the legacy of forty years of state socialism lingers on in Polish society as well as the economy. The new guard too often try to do business in Poland as if they were in the U.S.A. or Britain and come up against the reality of the emerging Polish market.

Entrepreneurs

It is hard to find an entrepreneurial spirit anywhere in Europe to match that of the Poles. The moment state restrictions on private business were eased in 1989, many started to put their savings into small businesses, ranging from produce stalls and hot-dog stands to nationwide franchises. This spirit has survived, buoyed partly by the high unemployment rates that force many to find other ways to make ends meet. For the moment, many small shops have weathered the storm of competition from supermarkets and international franchises. European Union integration, however, may make life increasingly difficult.

Biznesmen
The term *biznesman* is a label applied to Poland's more dubious entrepreneurs. The stereotypical Polish *biznesman* is involved in some sort of dodgy business, has very poor fashion sense, and will blow most of his fortune on a used, imported (most likely, stolen) BMW or Mercedes. The chances of a foreigner in the country on legitimate business meeting up with such a character are limited, but if you come across someone fitting this description, beware!

GREETINGS
When meeting someone for the first time in a business context, you should introduce yourself using both your first and last names and, regardless of gender, shake hands. Later, at a convenient moment, offer your business card. This is normally done sitting down at a table. Make sure that you have a card for everyone at the table, regardless of position. Generally the social conventions described in Chapter 4 apply.

MEETINGS

There is not much about business meetings in Poland that the visitor with a little intercultural experience would find odd or difficult to deal with. Coffee and tea are immediately offered by receptionists to any guests in the office, and it is common during a meeting to find  yourself sipping tea and nibbling on biscuits.

Protocol at meetings is relaxed. Normally the most senior person in attendance, or the person with whom you've had the most contact, will introduce those present and lay out the plan for the day. The agenda is normally presented verbally at this point.

Generally speaking, the atmosphere at meetings is also fairly relaxed. Poles feel free to speak their minds and often will. Foreigners should do the same or may be seen as weak or lacking ideas. If you have facts and figures to back up your points, ideas, or proposals, make sure you have them in a presentable format. Meetings in Poland are often called to present and discuss facts and findings, rather than to brainstorm new ideas.

Punctuality

Although it's never a bad thing to be on time, don't panic if you arrive ten minutes late for a business meeting in Poland. Punctuality is not a quality on which people are judged, although repeatedly showing up late may be seen as a reflection of your level of respect for the other party.

Don't Panic

An American businesswoman was taking part in a meeting held in a conference room at the Marriott Hotel in Warsaw. After problems with transportation, she arrived ten minutes late and entered the room out of breath, apologizing profusely. Those Polish participants who had already arrived (fewer than half) found it entertaining that anyone would panic over a mere ten minutes. They explained that the first fifteen minutes or so were used for mingling and small talk, only after which would business begin.

Presentations

Most Polish offices are well equipped with all the hardware you need for a presentation. Multimedia (Powerpoint style) presentations are becoming the norm in many companies. It always makes a good impression on Poles to fill a presentation with data and facts, although it may not be expected. Try to make eye contact with everyone present in the room, not just the most senior person. It is fine to start with a light anecdote, only be careful with jokes as cultural differences mean that your Polish audience may not find them as humorous as your colleagues back home. It is best to get down to business fairly quickly after starting. Finally, don't feel offended if you are interrupted—questions will be asked when they arise rather than kept till the end of the presentation.

Power Games

When invited to someone's office to meet face-to-face, it is not at all uncommon to be kept waiting from five to fifteen minutes. The receptionist is likely to tell you that the person you are to meet is with someone else or on the phone. In fact, this is a tactic often used to assert one's authority and to gain power in a relationship.

One power game not often used by Poles in meetings is that of sitting behind one's desk—the symbol of power—while the visitor sits opposite feeling awkward and powerless. Poles are far more likely to use a large, open table or a conference room, even for one-on-one meetings.

Where to Meet

Meetings generally take place in one's office. For group meetings it is common to rent a boardroom in a high-class hotel, which has the advantage of being a neutral location.

Lunch or dinner meetings are becoming increasingly common, but are used more as a way to cement good relations than to hammer out details. Business is discussed in the restaurant but in a rather informal manner and is intermixed with small talk. As in many other countries, the person who proposes the meeting will generally pay the bill, and it is seen as awkward to divide the bill in any way. If you would like to invite your Polish counterpart, ask someone, or indeed your guest, to recommend a good restaurant. Taking an interest in Polish cuisine will always be viewed favorably, as will taking advantage of the opportunity to learn more about Poland by asking your guest any questions you may have about the country. Don't be embarrassed about your ignorance of Polish history or culture—Poles love to enlighten visitors as to the situation, both past and present, in their country. Dinner meetings may last well into the night, and if they do it is an indication that business is going well. Breakfast meetings are still virtually unheard of.

Finding the Right Level of Formality
Finding the right level of formality in social situations in Poland can be tricky, and when business is involved it is of added importance.

Polish managers with international experience will be comfortable doing business in an informal manner and will generally follow your lead. If you are in a senior position, or older than your Polish counterpart, and prefer to work on a first-name basis then it is up to you to propose this. In the reverse situation it's better to hold off.

BUSINESS DRESS

Poland is not Silicon Valley and this is evident in the way businesspeople dress. Very few have the luxury of going to work in casual clothing and formal business dress is the norm. In Polish business, for better or worse, people are judged by their appearance. Furthermore, dressing well for a meeting shows your counterpart(s) that you value the opportunity to meet with them. A smart, stylish suit always makes a good impression. Having said this, some offices have recently implemented an American-style "casual Friday," allowing employees to show off their weekend wardrobes.

CORPORATE VERSUS LOCAL CULTURE

Exploiting the lack of a coherent, national business culture, many multinational companies operating in Poland have attempted to impose a strong corporate culture in the workplace. Such experiments have met with varying degrees of success. A strong corporate culture is often accepted by young, eager employees, wishing to make a career for themselves and move up in the organization. Older, more experienced, and better-educated employees tend to view such a regime as manipulative, and may react rather cynically to attempts to instill a strong corporate culture within the organization.

INTERCULTURAL MANAGEMENT
Many of the foreign managers in Poland have been working in their professions for longer than Poland has had a free market economy. By contrast, Polish managers tend to be much younger, with comparatively little international experience. It may seem natural then that the foreign managers see themselves as having superior knowledge and experience in comparison with their Polish colleagues. Without even realizing it, many Western managers may act in a manner that can be seen as patronizing to their Polish counterparts.

Despite the relative youth of many high-level managers in Poland, these are people who, for the most part, have worked very hard to earn their positions. Polish managers tend to be very well educated, and have an insight into the specific nuances of the Polish market that foreigners, regardless of their experience, cannot match. Western managers who realize that they can learn from their Polish colleagues, and who communicate this clearly, have the most fruitful business relations.

WESTERN ARROGANCE

Research by Central European University in Warsaw and the Free University of Berlin has shown that Polish managers consider arrogance on the part of Western managers to be one of the biggest obstacles to effective cooperation. In fact, what the Polish managers consider to be arrogance may simply be a lack of understanding of their way of doing things.

Communication

Communication is the key to avoiding such misunderstandings. Explaining why you would like a Polish colleague or subordinate to do something is as, or probably more, important than the task itself. Those foreign managers who have clear, regular communication with their Polish counterparts have the fewest problems.

In the case of a Western manager dealing with Polish subordinates, it is important to regularly check the progress of work and to do so in a supportive manner. A lack of such communication can lead to a situation where information is kept from you and your own colleagues and subordinates become uncooperative.

HIERARCHY
State-controlled companies in Communist times were extremely hierarchical. Not surprisingly, this organizational structure has survived in companies that are still state controlled, as well as those that, although privatized, have retained their senior management.

In this system, senior managers would secure their positions by surrounding themselves with loyal subordinates who restricted access to them by anyone outside the inner circle. Although this type of structure survives intact in relatively few companies, they tend to be very large and the structure very strong. When dealing with the employees of such a company, it is key to ascertain who the decision makers are and to deal directly with the highest-ranking person you can gain access to. This also applies to any dealings with government departments.

The reality in most companies is markedly different, although certain elements from the old system may survive. Western companies with young Polish managers tend to have a much less hierarchical structure where ideas and communication flow freely. Decision making may, however, still follow a very structured path.

PERSONAL CONTACTS

We have already noted that personal networks were crucial in the decades of Communism and still play an important role in modern Polish society. Nowhere is this more true than in business. Having contacts in the right places can help you to find products, people, and places, ease bureaucratic processes, speed up customs clearances, and generally make business more efficient. When someone tells you they have a friend who can help you, this is, in a sense, an introduction into an informal network.

Corruption and Bribery

There is no doubt that corruption exists on a large scale in Poland. For the foreigner doing business in Poland, the best advice is to keep to the moral high ground and not compromise yourself by paying bribes. Once you are seen to be willing to pay for certain favors it becomes expected.

Small "gifts" for personal favors are another matter, and much of what would be considered corrupt in other countries is considered normal business practice in Poland. If someone has assisted you with a problem in a way that would go beyond what you would expect of them (i.e., they have not been officially paid for this service) and you genuinely appreciate their assistance, then it is appropriate to offer a gift. This could be an invitation to dinner, a bottle of alcohol, or something from your own country, but not cash. Such presents are seen as gifts, whereas cash is seen as a bribe.

NEGOTIATING WITH POLES

There is no negotiating style that can be said to be specifically Polish. As with other aspects of business in Poland, much depends on the age and amount of international experience of the person with whom you are dealing. Once again, clear communication is the key. If your Polish counterpart has the impression that you are behaving in an arrogant fashion, or that you don't view them as an equal in your negotiations, they may react in a manner that can best be described as stubborn. Such behavior puts personal pride in front of the interests of the company, and can be terribly counterproductive.

On the whole, as long as you are clear and open in your negotiations, you can expect the same from the other side. Being a society where strong personal relations are important in business, a successful conclusion to your talks can be the first step in a strong and lasting partnership.

Closing Deals

There are no specific peculiarities regarding closing business deals in Poland. It is always a good idea nonetheless to have all agreements put down on paper, even if there is no formal agreement to be signed. This can simply be a letter of understanding that outlines the conclusions reached during negotiations as well as the obligations each party is to undertake.

Contracts

Contracts in business are respected and treated much as they would be in most Western countries. The standard process is that, following negotiations, one of the sides (probably the host) will have their lawyers draw up a draft contract. This will be sent to you and any objections or proposed changes will be taken seriously and another meeting called to discuss them if necessary. It is not common to come to such meetings with a team of lawyers, contract in hand, and pressurize for a signature.

All this having been said, however, some contracts, for example apartment rental contracts, are viewed as general guidelines more than a legally binding document. Huge delays in the courts make it impractical to pursue such matters and a compromise solution is normally sought. Although practically unenforceable, such contracts are mostly honored.

WOMEN IN BUSINESS

During the years of Communism, women had no difficulty with upward mobility in certain professions, but faced a brick wall in others. Today's situation is different. At the bottom rung of the ladder, women do not face discrimination by employers, nor are they held back from  promotion to low-level management. Here, however, the picture changes. Business is seen as a man's game, and women who make it to the boardroom may feel that they are not treated as equal partners, especially by elderly male directors and managers.

Statistically, women are paid less than men for the same work and are far less likely to be in the upper income brackets. A wife going to work is still viewed by many Poles, men and women alike, as a way to supplement the family income while the husband remains the breadwinner.

Legislation exists to protect women against sexual discrimination, but attitudes change slowly.

chapter nine

COMMUNICATING

THE POLISH LANGUAGE

The Polish language is a challenge for foreigners. Getting yourself around the clusters of consonants is a little like negotiating rush-hour traffic. Just try buying a train ticket to Szczecin and you'll get the point. Or how about telling a receptionist you'd like to speak with Krzysztof Brzeszczykiewicz? And it gets worse. Remember Latin lessons from school? Polish, like Latin, uses declensions, various noun forms that change according to the case. Polish grammar has seven cases and three genders and the result is a language that can be difficult even for native speakers. A simple example: the noun *dom*, meaning house, can be written *dom*, *domem*, or *domu*, depending on its use in the sentence. The same rule applies to proper nouns such as the names of towns, countries, and people.

One thing to keep you going through this linguistic labyrinth, however, is that your attempts to speak Polish, no matter how pathetic, will be appreciated. Poles are very proud of their language, and your attempts to use it will be seen as a sign of respect. Perhaps this is because very few people will actually expect you to make an effort. The Polish-language skills of many foreign businessmen are limited to ordering a drink, despite having lived in the country for years.

Do You Speak English? German? Russian?

Civil servants, railway employees, bus drivers, and others you may have to deal with are notoriously bad at foreign languages. There is a joke about two traffic policemen in Warsaw. An English businessman, completely lost and in need of help, sees them and pulls over:

"Do you speak English?" he asks.

"*Nie*," replies one of the officers.

"*Parlez vous francais?*"

"*Nie*," replies the other officer.

"*Gavareet pa Rusku?*"

"*Nie.*"

The Englishman, realizing he is not getting anywhere, rolls up his window and drives on. Later, the two policemen are speaking about the situation:

"Do you think we should learn a second language?" asks one.

"Why?" asks the other, "look at that foreigner, he speaks three and it doesn't help him."

Having said this, you will also find that many locals will be happy to have an opportunity to practice their English. There is the example of the foreign driver who was involved in a small car accident; even though he was at fault, the other driver was thrilled to have the chance to speak English as they exchanged insurance details.

The truth is that in major cities you can get by with English. When you need help with directions, menus, etc., look for someone under thirty and there's a good chance they'll be willing and able to assist you. Just remember to leave them with your best attempt at "*dziekuje*" ("Thank you").

Apart from English, German is fairly common in the west of the country and the Lake District (Mazury), as well as other parts that were historically part of Germany. German expatriates living in Poland say that there isn't any anti-German sentiment to speak of and they feel welcome in their neighbor's country.

If grudges from the Second World War are largely forgotten, the Cold War is another matter. Russian is widely understood, but attitudes among Poles to Russian speakers can vary greatly. Russian lessons were obligatory in Polish schools up to 1989, but have now been largely replaced by English, German, and French. Feelings about Russians are mixed. Many people seemed to be quite happy to watch the former big brother struggle economically and socially while at the same time Poland moved toward full E.U. membership.

CONVERSATION

Conversation is a joy for Poles and, in a friendly, informal setting, there is no need to feel inhibited about any topic. Even matters of religion or politics are not taboo. If any warning is needed it is in regard to criticism of Poland as a nation. As we have seen, the Poles find humor even in the darkest situations and often make jokes about their history or current situation. As a foreigner, however, you should avoid such comments about Poland. Jokes about your own country on the other hand will probably be enjoyed and help to remove the possibility of being viewed as an arrogant foreigner.

Volume

Poles like to be heard. Many foreigners visiting Poland for the first time wonder why people always seem to be arguing, but for Poles animated exchange is part of normal conversation. Don't feel offended therefore if a Polish friend or colleague disagrees with you in a very vocal and expressive manner. It actually means that you have been accepted as an active partner in the conversation. Nationally, politics and the economy are the topics you can expect Poles to be most vocal about although, depending on their interests, it could be any matter on which they have a strong opinion.

Body Language

It is not only in terms of volume that Poles are outwardly expressive. There is a joke that the best way to make a Spaniard stop talking is to tie up his hands, and while the same tactic may not mute a Pole, it would certainly cause a speech impediment. Unlike Southern Europeans, however, there is not as much significance placed in specific gestures. This is good news for foreigners as there is less chance of inadvertently causing offense or confusion by the misuse of a hand gesture.

Poles will often lean forward in their chair, or even stand up, in order to add weight to a specific point they are trying to make. It is also common, particularly in informal conversation between men, to touch the other's arm or give a pat on the back to make a point, gain attention, or show recognition or agreement.

Misunderstandings

Two such instances of misunderstandings caused by linguistic similarities are the meanings of the simple words "no" and "thank you."

The Polish word "no" is equivalent to the English conversation fillers "hmmm," "yeah," "well," or "really." It is used so habitually that even bilingual Poles may well use this expression when speaking English without even realizing it. Don't be surprised then if, for example, your comment that the restaurant you chose for lunch is very nice is met with a smiling "no" by your Polish guest.

"Thank you" ("*Dziekuje*") is another potential source of misunderstanding. Regarding a simple yes or no question, English speakers understand "thank you" to mean "yes," as in:
"Would you like a cup of tea?"
"Thank you."
Poles, however, regardless of what language is being used, would take this answer to mean "no." It is always best therefore to say "Yes please" or "No thank you." When asking such a question always make sure to ask for clarification when a Pole responds with "thank you."

Formal vs. Informal Forms of Address Revisited

As we have seen, finding the right level of formality can be difficult for foreigners dealing with Poles. Poles begin a new relationship, business or personal, on a very high level of formality, referring to each other as Sir or Madam (*pan/pani*). As there is no equivalent to this in modern English, simply use Mr. and Mrs. followed by the person's surname until they propose that you call them by their first name. If you are the elder person or hold a higher position (especially in business), it will be your responsibility to propose communicating on a first-name basis. Do this only when, and indeed if, you feel comfortable with it.

SENSE OF HUMOR

We have also seen that Poles like to laugh at themselves while at the same time retaining their pride in being Polish. This has complex social roots and foreigners should not attempt to join in jokes about Poland, which can be taken as criticism.

Polish humor is generally situation based. They like humor that is based on stories rather than wordplay, and find it strange that anyone can laugh at such simple things as someone falling over. American humor is seen by Poles as very simplistic and lacking in sarcasm and irony.

SWEARING

Swearing is common in Poland, although you probably won't understand any of it. As in most countries, however, who swears is important. Swearing can be a sign of someone's low social class and level of education although, having said that, in informal situations swearing is common among all classes of young Poles.

English swearwords and curses are widely known in Poland, as with most of the world, but do not carry the same weight as their equivalents in Polish. Don't be surprised therefore to hear such words or phrases used casually and out of context.

THE "YES" CULTURE

Many foreigners spending an extended period in Poland note a specific feature of Polish culture that can prove problematic. It seems that Poles prefer to say "yes" even when it may not be the most appropriate answer. This is especially the case for questions such as "Is everything going well with that project?" The truth may be that work on the project has barely started, but the answer "yes" reflects the optimism that everything will go well rather than the current situation. It is important to remember that for Poles this is not at all a dishonest or deceitful answer. For them, if someone was really interested in the progress of a project, they would ask specific questions about it. In fact, as this kind of response is part of their culture, Poles are completely unaware that it could be misunderstood. They have as difficult a time understanding your perception as you have theirs.

TELEPHONES AND *KOMORKI*

The state of the Polish telephone infrastructure is a far cry from the situation a mere ten years ago. Not so long ago many Poles were without a phone service, despite having had their names on waiting lists for ten years or more. Furthermore, getting a free, clear connection for a domestic call could prove difficult, let alone for an international line.

The situation today is much as in Western Europe with one key exception: price. Telecommunication rates in Poland are among the highest in Europe, and this is true for local, domestic, and international calls, as well as Internet connections through a modem.

Phone booths (*telefon na karty*) are easy to find, especially in large cities. To use a public telephone you'll need a phone card (*karta telefoniczna*). These are available in various denominations and can be purchased at a kiosk, post office, or hotel newsstand.

Area Codes
The international dialing code for Poland is 48. Area codes to some larger Polish cities are

presented in the following chart.

International dialing codes are, for the most part, the same throughout Europe and are usually written on, or next to, public telephones together with regional area codes.

POLAND AREA CODES
(inside Poland, begin with 0)
Gdansk 58
Katowice 32
Krakow 12
Poznan 61
Warsaw 22
Wroclaw 71

Komorki

Poland has a love affair with cellular phones, *telefony komorkowy*, known simply as *komorki*. In a relatively short period they have evolved from being status symbols to "must have" items, regardless of age and income. Businessmen, housewives, schoolchildren, and retired folk can all be seen strolling around town chatting on their cell phones. This is even more amazing given the prohibitive cost per minute to use or call cell phones in Poland.

There are three cellular phone networks in Poland and all operate on the GSM standard,

meaning that North American
cell phones will not work there,
while European phones with a
roaming option should work
problem free. If in Poland for an
extended period, it is easy for
foreigners to get a mobile phone
on a prepaid subscription basis. Cards to increase
the number of minutes available can be bought in
kiosks and post offices.

INTERNET AND E-MAIL

The Internet is certainly one of the areas where
Poland has not yet caught up with Western
Europe. Poland is rated among the least-wired
countries in Europe, with only 7 percent of Poles
having access to the Internet in 2003. If you come
to Poland with your laptop, don't expect a
plethora of "hot-spots" where you can enjoy free

wireless Internet access. In fact this is
a service that has only just begun,
with a few cafés and Western hotels
offering free "hot-spots." The good
news, however, is that there is an
ever-increasing number of
Internet cafés where you can use the
Internet and check your e-mail for very
reasonable rates. Polish Internet cafés range from

modern, high-tech places where, while surfing the net, you can enjoy a coffee, cold beer, or a snack to backroom operations mostly full of teenagers playing on-line games. Ask a young person in whichever town you're in and they will likely be able to point you in the direction of the nearest Internet café.

MAIL

The Polish postal system (*Poczta Polska*) is quite efficient and inexpensive. Post offices are located in practically every neighborhood and town and are normally open from 8:00 a.m. to 7:00 p.m., and all large cities have a post office open twenty-four hours. In addition to sending mail, you can purchase money orders, phone cards, and exchange currency.

Most post offices now have an automated number system to eliminate the long lines. Simply take a number from the dispensing machine upon entering, then wait for your number to be displayed above one of the windows. To send a letter or package by air mail, ask for *lotnicza* or the international standard, *par avion*. You must also affix a blue *lotnicza* sticker, which you will find in baskets on all counters. Unfortunately it is unlikely that you will find anyone working at the post office who can assist you in English.

MEDIA

Poles are and have always been avid
newspaper readers. Since the fall of
Communism the full spectrum of
political opinion has been
available. The leading newspaper is
the *Gazeta Wyborcza* ("Election
Gazette"), edited by the Solidarity member Adam
Michnik. And if you can't read Polish, there are
three established English-language magazines to
help you out. The *Warsaw Voice*, *Warsaw Insider*,
and *Warsaw Business Journal* all offer up-to-date
information for expatriate residents and tourists in
the capital. In addition there are various free
tourist information magazines available in English
from hotels, airports, train stations, and tourist
information centers.

CONCLUSION

As we have seen, Poland retains much from its
history, both ancient and recent. The changes that
have swept through the large cities in the last
twenty years have left much of the countryside,
where life moves at a far slower pace, seemingly
untouched. However, all of Poland's history—the
glory and the oppression, stagnation and
resurgence—has been absorbed into the country's
cultural fabric.

Although modern Poland may lack cultural diversity, its cosmopolitan past has left its mark, with Germans, Jews, French, Italians, Russians, and Tatars all leaving traces in Polish art, architecture, cuisine, folklore, and myth.

Individual Poles, such as Copernicus, Marie Curie, Frederic Chopin, Joseph Conrad, and Roman Polanski, have contributed greatly to Western science and culture. As a nation, Poland gave the world one of its first written constitutions and, more importantly, the knowledge that a people can endure any hardship and start again to rebuild their lives and their country.

This book offers you a cultural compass, to help you discover for yourself something of the richness of the Polish experience and way of life. Your journey will be both exciting and rewarding.

Appendix: Some Useful Web Sites

U.S. Library of Congress Country Report—Poland
http://lcweb2.loc.gov/frd/cs/pltoc.html

A comprehensive background on Polish geography, economy, society, and history. Very thorough, but not very up-to-date. A great fact file.

CIA World Factbook—Poland
www.cia.gov/cia/publications/factbook/geos/pl.html

Another excellent source for concrete facts in a quick reference format.

Official Polish government Web site (in English)
www.poland.gov.pl/

A user-friendly site offering an interesting introduction to the country and its people.

Polonia Today
www.poloniatoday.com

The self-proclaimed "world's most read Polish-American newsmagazine in the English language."

Poland.com
www.poland.com/

A great source for hotels, flights, tours, and car rentals.

PKP—Polish National Railway homepage (available in English)
www.pkp.pl

Check the Inter-City and local train timetables.

Orbis—National hotel company and tour operator (available in English)
www.orbis.pl

Book hotels and tours.

LOT–Polish National Airline
www.lot.com

Check the schedule and book international and domestic flights.

Warsaw Voice—**English-language weekly newspaper**
www.warsawvoice.pl/

A good source for keeping up-to-date with current events in Poland.

Warsaw Insider—**English-language monthly magazine**
www.warsawinsider.pl/

This magazine has a great index of restaurants, pubs, cafés, theaters, etc. as well as ex-pat clubs and organizations.

Warsaw Business Journal—**English-language business weekly**
www.wbj.pl/

Business and general news as well as good restaurant reviews.

Further Reading

Czerniewicz-Umer, Teresa, Malgorzata Omilanowska, and Jerzy S. Majewski. *Poland* (Eyewitness Travel Guides). New York: DK Publishing Inc., 2003.

Davies, Norman. *God's Playground*. Volume 2. New York: Columbia University Press, 1982.

Davies, Norman. *Heart of Europe: The Past in Poland's Present*. Oxford: Oxford University Press, 2001.

Davies, Norman. *Rising '44: The Battle for Warsaw*. New York: Viking Books, 2004.

Dydynski, Krzysztof. *Poland, A Travel Survival Kit*. Hawthorn, Australia: Lonely Planet Publications, 2002.

Knab, Sophie Hodorowicz. *Polish Customs, Traditions, and Folklore*. New York: Hippocrene Books, 1996.

Lukowski, Jerzy, and Hubert Zawadski. *A Concise History of Poland*. Cambridge: Cambridge University Press, 2001.

Michener, James. *Poland*. New York: Fawcett Books, 1990.

Olson, Lynne, and Stanley Cloud. *A Question of Honor: The Kosciuszko Squadron: Forgotten Heroes of World War II*. New York: Knopf, 2003.

Salter, Mark. *The Rough Guide to Poland*. London: Rough Guides, 2002.

Szpilman, Wladyslaw. *The Pianist: The Extraordinary True Story of One Man's Survival in Warsaw, 1939–1944*. New York: Picador, 2002.

Terterov, Marat, and Jonathan Reuvid (eds). *Doing Business with Poland* (Global Market Briefings). London: Kogan Page, 2002.

Zamoyski, Adam. *The Polish Way: A Thousand-Year History of the Poles and Their Culture*. New York: Hippocrene Books, 1993.

Index